THE MARRIAGE GAP

THE MARRIAGE GAP

A Psychologist Probes the Divorce
Explosion—and Comes up with some
Surprising Thoughts About Why
Marriages Are Breaking Apart
(and Why Some Don't Have To
and Others Should)

by **STANLEY ROSNER, Ph.D.**
and **LAURA HOBE**

David McKay Company, Inc.

NEW YORK

To my husband, John, with love and gratitude.

L. H.

To David, Elisa, Adam, and Jennifer—to their future and the marriages in their future.

S. R.

LIBRARY OF CONGRESS CATALOG CARD NUMBER: 73–84055

ISBN 0–679–50408–7

MANUFACTURED IN THE UNITED STATES OF AMERICA

Contents

Contents

PART I

MARRIAGE—WHAT IS IT, AND WHO NEEDS IT?

1

If the Bumps on Her Head
Fit the Holes in His . . .

Al and Jean have been married for eighteen years. They have three children, an above-average income, and live in the suburbs of a large city. From what their friends could see, they got along very well until recently, although everyone wondered how Jean put up with Al's overbearing behavior. He was not only the boss in the family, but the king, the tyrant, and supreme commander. Each morning before he left for work he wrote out assignments for Jean and the children, and each evening he checked to see that his orders had been properly carried out.

Jean was a submissive woman who didn't seem to mind being more of a servant than a wife. She did everything Al wanted, and if he wasn't satisfied, she never objected when he criticized her. If he ridiculed her in front of their friends, she didn't protest.

About two years ago, Jean learned that Al had had a very brief affair, and since then their marriage hasn't been the same. It wasn't that Jean was jealous, nor did she want to leave her husband; but she was no longer quite as willing to tolerate Al's dictatorial behavior. When he gave too many orders, she told him she didn't have time to bother with them. If he complained about the way she did things, she told him to do them himself.

Neither Al nor Jean want a divorce, at least not yet. But they are clearly unhappy.

What happened to this marriage? What held it together for so long, and why did it begin to come apart? These questions could be asked of many marriages.

Do you ever wonder what some married people see in each other? Or why some "perfect" marriages come apart? Do you know what *really* makes a happy marriage? Do you have questions about your own marriage? That's what this book is all about.

A man and a woman are drawn together by their needs and by their ability to fulfill them in each other. These needs are not always rational, however, nor are they always known to the man and woman themselves. If Al and Jean, for instance, had been aware of the real reasons why they needed each other, their marriage would have been quite different.

For a few years before she met Al, Jean had led a loose, rebellious life. She came from a puritanical, straitlaced family who seemed cold and unresponsive to her need for love and affection. While she didn't dare rebel at home, she had her fling when she went away to college. As she put it, "It was as if someone else got hold of me—I still can't believe I was doing those things." She drank a lot, slept around, and got a reputation for being loose. When she became aware of what she was doing, she was terrified at her lack of self-control. That's when she met Al.

Al had a lot of the same impulses Jean had. He, too, had been brought up by strict parents who showed him very little affection. His father, a minister of a fundamentalist church, forbade him to dance, smoke, drink, or even to think of girls. "When I was in my early teens and started having sexy fantasies about girls," Al recalls, *"why, I was convinced I was going straight to hell."* Al's mother was an aloof, quiet, undemonstrative woman who did little more than follow her husband's orders. Unlike Jean, Al maintained a tight control over his behavior.

When Al met Jean he was already out of college and working his way up in a large company. To Jean he seemed like the Rock of Gibraltar—a bit square, perhaps, but a welcome change from the anxious undergraduates she had known. The primary reason for her attraction to him, however, was something she couldn't acknowledge consciously: Al could keep her in line. He could provide the control she felt she lacked. He could save her from herself.

Al didn't know about Jean's past and he made no attempt to find out. To his conscious mind she seemed like a nice girl from a nice family, and he wanted her for his wife. A more important reason, but one that was not known to him on a conscious level, was that he sensed Jean's promiscuous impulses and got a vicarious pleasure out of them. For years he had unconsciously wished he could let loose, smoke and dance, drink and go with a lot of girls, but he had never dared risk his father's wrath. Nor could he admit that these impulses still lingered in his unconscious mind. Consciously, he tried to preserve the image of the upstanding young man. Jean could help him do this and at the same time satisfy the hidden promiscuous appetites he couldn't face in himself.

For most of their eighteen years of marriage Jean's need to be controlled and Al's need to control gave them the satisfaction they wanted. By giving Jean orders and assignments, Al was also keeping his own inner impulses in check. By carrying out Al's orders, Jean was safe from her own desires. Need was meeting need.

Finally the pressure exerted by Al's unconscious impulses became too much for him to control. Briefly and momentarily he broke loose and had an affair. While the other woman meant nothing *to him, the rigid relationship of his marriage was shattered. To Jean, Al had exposed a weakness, which meant that he was no longer the Rock of Gibraltar she needed. To make matters worse, Al began to drink. If he couldn't control himself, how could he control her? To Al, his brief acknowledgment of his inner needs tore away at his righteous image of himself.*

In each of these partners there was a gap between their conscious desires and their unconscious impulses. Al and Jean could not face up to their inner needs, and so they had been using each other—and their marriage—to cover them up and at the same time to satisfy or to frustrate them. This kind of a marriage works as long as the partners' original needs and responses remain the same. But, as we have seen, once the needs or the responses of one partner change, the entire relationship is disrupted—and not necessarily by the event that appears to cause all the trouble.

Sometimes people mature under the strain of a disrupted marriage. Jean, in testing and confronting her overbearing husband, is discovering that she now can depend on her own sense of self-control. Al is learning that his tyranny of others doesn't guarantee his control of himself. Both are learning that their inner needs represent normal appetites and desires that can be satisfied in a mature relationship without the surrender of self-control. Eventually this husband and wife may be able to acknowledge their inner needs and seek out each other out on that level. If not, the marriage will probably end.

This book is about marriages, the good ones and the bad ones. For we believe that it is just as important to know what makes a marriage happy as to know what makes it miserable.

As long as men and women are strangers to their innermost needs, as long as they are unable or unwilling to come to grips with the stresses and strains within themselves, they will bring these stresses and strains with them into their marriages. These are the bad marriages, the broken marriages, the marriages that make people wonder whether there is anything good about the institution of marriage itself.

But when men and women are aware of their deepest needs, when they understand themselves and know what they want from each other, and when they choose their mates to fulfill these needs—then there is no wide gap in the marriage because there is no wide gap within the partners. These are the better marriages, the ones that are apt to last, the ones that allow the partners to grow, individually and together. And a good marriage is the highest, most rewarding, worthwhile form of human intimacy.

2

What Kinds of Beds Do We Make?

It was a group therapy meeting in the office of a met-ropolitan-area psychotherapist. The discussion drifted, as it often did, to marital problems, which was something all members of the group had in common.

One man, who had been in therapy longer than any of the others, complained bitterly about his wife, who, he said, was sexually unresponsive, domineering, and com-pletely unsympathetic to his problems.

"Why don't you leave her?" another man snapped, impatient at hearing this same old story again.

"Because I'm already on my second marriage, and I just don't want to have to go on to a third."

In the office of a suburban law firm, a divorce attorney asked a middle-aged woman if she was planning to re-marry after her divorce was granted. "Hell, no!" she said. "I've had enough of that trap!" Two days after her divorce was granted, she was married again.

At a wedding reception in the social center of a large,

new church built into the side of a western mountain range, a young bride's cousin asked her why she had changed her mind about marriage. "I thought you weren't going to get tied down, *ever!*" she reminded the bride.

"I know," the bride shrugged. "Here's where the fun ends for me."

In a small rural church in the Middle West a young man and woman, both in jeans and warm horse-blanket-plaid jackets, stood before a minister and spoke the vows they had written for their wedding ceremony. They had lived together for almost a year, part of the time as members of a commune, and when a relative asked them why they were bothering to legalize their union, they said simply, "Because we want to—we want the commitment."

Another young couple, both of whom planned to finish college, got married in their junior year because they "couldn't stand being apart any longer." They lived in one room, survived mostly on tunafish casseroles, worked at part-time jobs to make their frayed ends meet, and tried to keep up with their classes. But it was hard. The money just wasn't there, and it looked as if one of them would have to drop out of school and get a job. Which one it was going to be, they couldn't decide. Each felt an education was essential to future success, and each was eager to begin a career.

Why did these men and women get married? Why did the man in group therapy feel that he would *have* to go into a third marriage if two previous marriages had failed? Why did the woman who was so bitter about her first marriage try again? Why did a young girl get married when to her it meant the end of all the good times in life? What did the couple mean by "commitment" when they didn't have a place to live or any means of support? And if an education was so important to the college couple, why didn't they live together on campus and get married *after* they graduated?

It would have been much better for these couples, in their particular circumstances, if they hadn't married. Probably they weren't ready for marriage, and in some cases they never would be. Yet they committed themselves to a binding relationship that would be difficult to sever. Their reasons were complex, often hidden from themselves and each other, and as varied as the persons involved. But they were not the kinds of reasons that lead to a good and lasting marriage.

It is natural for men and women to seek intimacy with each other, but not everyone is capable of achieving such a relationship. Nevertheless, couples continue to marry on the basis of what they imagine they want from each other, which often is far from what they can ever hope to get. Eventually their disillusionment becomes a primary cause of divorce. For an even greater number of marriages it creates an environment of misery that should, but doesn't, end in divorce.

Marriage is a wonderful human relationship—*if* people are ready for it. But too many couples aren't, and so they marry for the wrong reasons. Some simply want to get away from their parents and don't have the self-confidence to do it on their own; or, as one bride put it, "Isn't marriage great! You don't have to tell anyone where you're going or where you've been." Some expect marriage itself to provide everything they hope to achieve as individuals. When their goals don't materialize, the marriage is blamed more often than the individuals. Consequently, we are hearing more and more about altering the institution of marriage or doing away with it completely. Neither of these suggestions, however, is a workable approach to the growing number of problems we are encountering in marriage today. They are the angry outcries of disappointed people who did not, and do not, know what marriage is all about in the first place.

What is marriage?

Marriage is simultaneously the most rewarding yet the most demanding relationship two people can achieve. It is definitely for adults, and that has very little to do with the chronological ages of the husband and wife. Marriage is a mature relationship that can be shared only by mature people. Simply being a man or a woman is not enough of a qualification. Maturity, however, is not characteristic of a great many of the people who are saying "I do."

"I do"—*what?* How many brides and grooms could answer that question? The words in the traditional marriage ceremonies make a lot of promises and build up a lot of expectations, but they have become so familiar to most of us that they have lost their meaning. Love . . . honor . . . cherish . . . comfort, forsaking all others . . . in sickness and in health . . . they've become charming words in a charming ritual that brides and grooms chant but rarely comprehend. They *sound* pretty, and if any of the words don't please our ears, we change them. We can't rearrange marriage so easily.

Through marriage we are seeking the things we need to feel complete as persons—closeness and intimacy with another human being, acceptance of what we are and appreciation of what we are to become, sexual delight and fulfillment, communication of our feelings and thoughts on the deepest levels of our beings, commitment to a shared love and a shared life, the exclusive belonging to and devotion of the person we love.

It is also through marriage that we meet our needs as members of society. We form families into which a new generation is born, educated, civilized, and enabled to mature. Today, not every couple chooses to have children; nevertheless, the man-and-woman partnership is a family unit of interrelated persons who are able to function as a whole—having its own dwelling, its own way of life, its goals; producing, consuming, creating; this is how we fulfill not only our own needs, but those of others. The family unit is the dynamic foundation upon which our social structure rests and will continue to rest for an indeterminate future time.

Obviously this is not a description that fits many marriages today. It more accurately describes what marriage can be. But between it and what exists for many couples is the chasm we call the Marriage Gap. This describes the difference between what the couple say they want in marriage and what their *real* needs are. It represents the conflict between the conscious and the unconscious in our individual selves and the effect of this conflict on our relationships. Here, in this gap, is where so many marriages go wrong—and the gap is growing.

The structure of marriage is changing faster and more radically than at any time in our history. The roles of husband and wife are becoming less defined as men and women are breaking free of their traditional molds. The husband is no longer the sole moneymaker; the wife is no longer the sole homemaker. Women are restless as they seek new ways to fulfill themselves as individuals rather than as a part of the man. Men are confused not only by the new women, but by a technologically dominated way of life that offers them no traditional masculine identity. It's a time of sexual uncertainty as well as exploration.

Marriage has always reflected major changes in our social, economic, political, and individual lives, and we can expect these changes to occur even faster in the future. But the changes will affect the behavior patterns of husbands and wives more than the function of marriage itself. Men and women will still come together to fulfill their deep mutual needs for each other. However, when changes in our environment occur so rapidly, they make it more difficult for men and women to discover who they are and what they need from each other. It becomes harder for them to distinguish between appearance and reality, and mistakes can be made more frequently. It's especially unfortunate when marriage becomes one of their most painful errors.

Throughout history marriage has been misunderstood and misused. Perhaps the greatest fallacy associated with it has been the conviction that *everyone* should get married, and the sooner the better.

For centuries marriage was considered a religious, social, and cultural necessity. Indeed, it *was* an economic necessity, and not only for women. Having no other choice but to marry, men and women had to live with any mistakes they made in selecting a mate, for there was little hope for a second chance. Perhaps that's why certain myths developed and were passed down from one generation to the next:

There was something wrong with you if you didn't get married—and you were plain crazy if you didn't *want* to.

You didn't have to love your mate (or even know him or her very well)—that would come in time.

Marriage problems could be solved if you tried hard enough.

All marriages could and should be saved.

None of these assumptions is true, and we no longer need to deceive ourselves with them, but we're having a hard time working our way free of their influence. Today, although our personal lives are less restricted by religious dogma, social rigidity, or by narrow economic and cultural opportunities, we still hesitate to call these old marriage "truths" by their proper name—*Nonsense!* Perhaps, though, they still serve a need in that they cover up the real—and self-destructive—reasons why so many of us marry badly.

Now, for the first time in history, we have an opportunity to become objective about marriage; to see what makes it work and what turns it into hell on earth; to determine who among us is ready for marriage and who would be happier in a less demanding, less committed relationship, at least until he or she is ready to share a fully mature union. Ironically, however, while our greater personal freedom enables marriage to reach its potential as an enriching human experience, it also threatens marriage with complete deterioration so long as we move ahead into the future under the influence of past compulsions.

What marriage has been

Marriage as we know it evolved over many centuries. Primitive men and women probably followed their affinities and chose their own mates. When it became apparent that coupling was a good way to combine a fortune, as in the case of two prosperous families, or to make a fortune, as in the case of a young man who managed to snare a bride with a large dowry, mating became a business matter negotiated by families, with or without the consent of the prospective marriage partners. Quite often the bride and groom met each other for the first time on their wedding day and, affinity or no affinity, they were expected to make a go of their marriage. If they didn't get along, the families intervened to restore harmony. Separation or divorce in such unions was almost out of the question, for it would have involved complicated redistributions of family wealth. It would also bring on the wrath of the church, which in those days had a formidable economic clout of its own.

Marriages were also arranged for social reasons. For instance, in the nineteenth century a penniless young woman or man whose blood was the proper shade of blue had a decent chance of marrying into an ambitious, affluent, industrial family hungry for aristocratic ties. Ethnic solidarity was another reason for family-arranged marriages. Again, couples were expected to make the best of their lot, even if it meant seeking their happiness in a discreet affair or two. The trauma associated with divorce in John Galsworthy's Forsyte family may seem almost farcical to us now, but it is a true representation of Victorian attitudes.

Marriage was altered by the Industrial Revolution, although the effects weren't evident until early in the twentieth century. Whole populations began to shift, with men and women going where the jobs were. The salary gave them independence, mobility, security, and choice. Fortunes could be improved, even created, by a person's skill and wits rather than by one's marriage prospects. The pressure-strength of multigeneration families was fragmented as the younger members sought careers far from the traditional family home. With greater distance between the offspring and the enforcers of family customs, young men and women began to exercise their own choice in the selection of a mate.

Some students of history believe that mating by personal choice destroyed the stability of marriage, for only then did separation, divorce, and successive marriages become more evident. They argue that husbands and wives in family-arranged marriages were happier in the long run because: a) being forced to lie in a bed they didn't make, they at least tried to make it comfortable, or, in the words used so often today, "they worked at their marriage"; and b) their parents, being objective, were more capable of selecting compatible marriage partners. While there is some truth in these claims, there is also the probability that many husbands and wives in family-arranged marriages were very unhappy and would have gone their separate ways if they had been free to do so without facing social ostracism. Some of the choices made by the families were no doubt better than those the spouses might have made on their own, but it could have been only by accident that these husbands and wives were able to satisfy, or even comprehend, each other's inner needs. As couples they put up a good front, but occasional recorded remarks give us a hint of what really went on.

The poet Menander, speaking for the ancient Greeks, said, "Marriage, if one will face the truth, is an evil, but a necessary evil."

Shakespeare had Othello refer to marriage as "a curse," and John Heywood, a near-contemporary of Shakespeare, came right out and compared marriage to hanging:

> Wedding is destiny,
> And hanging likewise.

"Marriage is a desparate thing," said John Selden a little later, and Swinburne offered this depressing evaluation:

> Marriage and death and division
> Make barren our lives.

The fact that marriages lasted longer in past ages doesn't mean that marriages were better or happier than they can be today. One aspect of arranged marriages we overlook is the support and security an established family could give to a couple. If a man and woman didn't get along, older members of the family intervened in an attempt to bring them together. In other words, the family had its built-in marriage counselors. While these efforts didn't always bring about a real healing in cases of a deep rift between husband and wife, they probably prevented the kind of impulsive separations that are caused by superficial differences—and certainly we have a lot of those in our society.

Differences that couldn't be resolved had to be endured, which means that those "stable" marriages often were achieved at the expense of the spouses. Today we would hardly be so complacent about a person's right to a happy life.

What kind of beds do we make?

We can't deny the evidence, however, that as our personal freedom has increased, we have been making a mess of marriage. The mistakes of the past may have been buried with the past, but ours are out in the open. Statistics indicate that although we keep getting married, we can't stay married. Why?

Part of the answer can be found in our changing society and its impact on our life-styles. Our traditions and values are being reshaped by affluence, by flexible sexual mores made possible by the Pill and legalized abortion, by looser religious and family ties, by urbanization and the geographic mobility that goes with it. We buy more and move around more; we have shorter relationships with many more people and tend to expect less from them. We can lose ourselves and our identity in a crowd or in a totally new environment; we aren't overly concerned about such things as reputation or our standing in a community because the chances are we won't remain in the same community for very long. We can start life over as many times as we choose. We don't *have* to get married, or stay married—we can afford divorce.

Another part of the answer can be found in the changing roles of men and women. The willingness of women to take on greater responsibility for their lives has made them more demanding of marriage. In the process of becoming the true equals of men they are no longer able to squeeze themselves into a marital role they had no part in designing. If an existing marriage can't meet their emerging needs, the marriage must go—and perhaps a new one will take its place.

The liberated woman's problems are fairly clear-cut. But women who are influenced by the liberation movement, yet unable to fit into it, may have greater difficulties in their marriage. The woman who wants to be treated like a little girl and at the same time enjoy the advantages of independence, makes it impossible for a man to satisfy her needs. These are the marriages that are more likely to be damaged by the readjustment of male and female roles.

Men, too, have problems with their identity. As women become breadwinners, as they perform more of the same kind of work men do, as they enjoy the same sexual freedom, many men feel threatened. Their insecurity is bound to show up in their marriages.

One of the casualties of our fast-paced society is the human-to-human relationship. This is the day of the alienated person who finds it safer and less painful to keep his distance from others. Because he is out of touch with his own emotions and needs, he has little desire to contact the emotional core of another human being. Relationships formed on superficial levels are likely to break apart under stress.

Ours is a "disposable" society. We have an amazing range of choices before us, and if one life-style doesn't work, we can get rid of it. That's what is happening to many marriages.

Fewer men and women are getting married and expecting it to last forever. Some men and women are suggesting that marriage itself should change in order to accommodate the changes in our life-styles. They feel that marriage as we now know it prevents each spouse from becoming an independent, fulfilled person. As a solution, they propose an "open marriage" kind of relationship in which a husband and a wife are free to go their own ways within the framework of marriage. Neither must defer to the other, and each does as he or she pleases, alone or together. In other words, rather than living together on a 50/50 basis, they live on a 100/100 basis. It's questionable, however, whether this arrangement would be a marriage at all. In a 50/50 relationship, two people share, whereas in a 100/100 relationship, they give nothing to each other.

Since there is no reason why marriage should stand in the way of human fulfillment, the question for men and women to answer—before they get married—is whether or not they want to share their fulfillment with another person. Nobody says they must.

Underlying all these social stresses on married life today is a more important reason for marital breakdown: marriage is for mature people and too many men and women are getting married before they have had a chance to grow up emotionally. Intimacy, for instance, means different things to different people, depending upon their emotional age level. The fully developed adult sees intimacy as a shared, loving relationship with another fully developed adult, both of whom will continue to grow as individuals and as partners. The immature person is more often looking for a substitute parent-figure to fill the void created by the deficiencies of the real parent who, for one reason or another, failed to give the child the emotional nourishment he or she needed in order to grow. These people seek a dependent relationship that will enable them to remain as children. The very prospect of growth threatens them with adult problems and responsibilities they cannot handle.

Undoubtedly, it was the hope of finding a parent (or

of playing the parent, which is another attempt to replace the parent figure) that led the group therapy member to think of marriage as a necessity in his life. The same can be said of the divorced woman who saw marriage as a trap, the bride whose good times were over, the couple who wanted "commitment," and the couple who eventually would have to choose between marriage and an education. All of them, each in his and her own way, were trying to fulfill immature needs by means of a relationship only a mature couple can hope to achieve. Their unconscious demands and expectations not only conflicted with the vows they were making to each other in the name of a ceremony, but their needs were unreasonable and often impossible to fulfill. From the very beginning, these marriages—and their number is increasing, judging from the types of problems psychotherapists are being asked to treat—are doomed to failure of one kind or another. Some of them will increase the already swelling divorce figures. Many more will be kept alive, but unhappy, by the fact that the partners are catering to each other's infantile needs. These marriages—in which the partners resist growth, together or individually; in which each eyes the other with apprehension and distrust; in which each fears that his or her real (and undeveloped) self will be disclosed and therefore cannot dare to communicate what is felt; in which neither one can give to the other, or take from the other; in which each blames the other for his unhappiness, but in which neither can give up the other—these are the most pitiful marital failures we see today.

If our immaturities and infantile needs were more evident, many of us could avoid a bad marriage. Certainly none of the people we mentioned earlier would have married had they realized why they were doing it and how slim were their chances for success. But many of us don't know ourselves well at all, and very often we resist the truth when it is in plain sight.

Most people play the role of the adult, even if they don't feel it. This, in fact, is another reason why so many immature men and women rush into marriage—they want to complete the role they have created for themselves and they see marriage as the badge of adult accomplishment.

To people who don't really feel they are grown men and women, this role-playing is essential in all their relationships. It hides from themselves and others the fact that emotionally they are little children. And so they are trapped between two opposing needs: that of playing the part of the adult, in the hope that no one will guess how inadequate they are, and that of answering the demands of the child within them. For the child cannot be silenced. Here, on the unconscious level, are the basic drives that will shape that person's life. Compared to the power and urgency of these drives, the assumed role and needs that are given lip service on the conscious level of a person's life are feeble.

As we will see in later chapters, a mature person is close to his feelings, and there is little difference or conflict between his or her conscious and unconscious needs. He or she is ready to interrelate with another mature person, so that they can achieve life's highest form of fulfillment—the mutual satisfaction of their deepest desires. This is what marriage is all about. If it does not satisfy, or if it is used to serve childish needs, then it isn't marriage.

The immature person says he wants the same thing a mature person wants, but on the unconscious level of his being he really wants something quite different. He's like the man who skips meals because he says he wants to lose weight, but in between eats everything in sight. While dieting fits into the role he's playing, he must stuff the hungry, demanding child within him. In marriage, the immature person will attempt to satisfy his inner, irrational needs by unconsciously frustrating the needs he pretends to have. For instance, a man who needs to be dependent, who fears that he cannot compete with more mature men, will find ways to be fired from a job he thinks he cannot handle. While he may complain about the scarcity of jobs and the prejudice of potential employers, and while he may weep loudly over the fact that his wife has to support the family, he is satisfying his need to be a little boy holding onto his mother's skirts. Similarly, the woman who complains that her husband spends most of his life at the office may really be nagging him into staying away from home so that she can continue to fit her image of herself as the neglected child.

Between the conscious and unconscious needs of spouses is the Marriage Gap. The wider the distance between what a person thinks and says he needs and what he's really after, the greater the tension within him. And that tension will be carried over into his relationship with his spouse. Add to this marriage the pressures from our fast-changing culture and the possibility that one or both partners may outgrow their childish need for the other, and you can see why there are so many more divorces today. However, there are also more marriages.

Going back only a few years we can see how the number of divorces has been growing. According to figures taken from United States census reports, there were 393,000 divorces in 1960, 479,000 in 1965, and 768,000 in 1971. Quite a jump. But in 1960 there were 1,523,000 marriages, in 1965 there were 1,800,000, and in 1971 there were 2,196,000!

Is marriage obsolete?

What these figures reflect, in part, is the way human behavior is changing in response to a changing world. Never before has the individual had so many opportunities from which to choose. He can pretty well become whatever he pleases, depending upon which of his needs he chooses to satisfy. He can live where he pleases, do the kind of work he prefers, be as successful as he wants to be, form whatever kind of relationships are best for him and for as long as he wishes. There are no strings attached to his life unless he puts them there.

As he chooses, he changes. As he becomes aware of new facets of life, his interests and his thoughts and his activities change. What he chooses may not only satisfy his needs but may arouse needs he never knew he had. The marriage that once satisfied him may now frustrate him. The partner who used to stimulate may now stifle. He meets new people all the time, and as he changes he may find that someone else satisfies his needs more completely than the partner he already has. And he is free— socially, religiously, economically, and morally—to choose between them.

Many people, faced with these opportunities to do their thing, feel that their choices would be limited by marriage. Some of them have indeed been handicapped within the kind of marriage where two people compete with, rather than reinforce, each other. In these cases, a divorce means not so much the breakdown of the marriage as the liberation of one of the spouses.

Marriage used to satisfy a person's need for a stable, permanent relationship. While that need still exists in men and women today, it is somewhat overshadowed by many other personal needs that can now, for the first time, be given attention. Society has at last arrived at the point where each person feels free to develop himself, to explore and express his talents and generally to see just how far he can go with them. He does not feel obligated to surrender this right, or even a part of it, to anyone. For this reason, many men and women are questioning whether they should marry at all.

In spite of their insistence on personal fulfillment, however, more people are getting married. Their marriages may not last very long, and often do not seem to give the partners what they are seeking from an intimate relationship, but they are taking place at a greater rate than ever.

What we have, then, is a growing number of men and women who feel that marriage cheats them out of their opportunities to develop themselves. Many of them believe they must make a choice between their own fulfillment and their desire to share life with someone they love. While many are choosing to marry, if the marriage doesn't last they are convinced that they made the wrong choice. Actually, their view of marriage as a threat to fulfillment may have been one of the very reasons for their marital failure, in that they were unable to share.

There is no reason to believe that we must choose between self-fulfillment and sharing life with a loved one. The outcome of the relationship really will depend upon the relative development of the men and women who enter marriage. For example, the hung-up single person will very likely bring his hang-ups into his marriage, whereas the person who has true freedom of choice—something that comes from within—will not feel the least bit trapped when sharing his life with another person.

As attractive as the single life appears to be today, it has its problems. As any psychotherapist can testify, the single person may feel as trapped by his circumstances as the married person. He may be handicapped by an inability to form the kind of lasting, intimate relationship that leads to marriage. Or he may find his "freedom of choice" limited by his reluctance to accept the responsibility that is part of independence.

The high incidence of divorce and remarriage leads some people to conclude that marriage is going out of style. Some critics believe that it will eventually disappear from our way of life. It will be replaced, they say, by short-term, uncommitted relationships formed according to the temporary needs of the partners.

As long as men and women need what marriage can offer them (which is the same as saying, as long as they are human), they will get married. And as long as men and women *think* they want this relationship when they aren't ready for it, we will have broken marriages.

If at first we don't succeed, we keep on trying—perhaps forever—and this pattern seems more likely to dominate the marriage of the future. In *Future Shock* Alvin Toffler sees this accelerated repetition of marriage-divorce-remarriage becoming a life-style:

As human relationships grow more transient and modular, the pursuit of love becomes, if anything, more frenzied. But the temporal expectations change. As conventional marriage proves itself less and less capable of delivering on its promise of lifelong love, therefore, we can anticipate open public acceptance of temporary marriages. Instead of wedding "until death do us part," couples will enter into matrimony knowing from the first that the relationship is likely to be short-lived.

They will know, too, that when the paths of husband and wife diverge, when there is too great a discrepancy in developmental stages, they may call it quits—without shock or embarrassment, perhaps even without some of the pain that goes with divorce today. And when the opportunity presents itself, they will marry again . . . and again . . . and again.

Serial marriage—a pattern of successive temporary marriages—is cut to order for the Age of Transience in which all man's relationships, all his ties with the environment, shrink in duration. It is the natural, the inevitable outgrowth of a social order in which automobiles are rented, dolls traded in, and dresses discarded after one-time use. It is the mainstream marriage pattern of tomorrow.

And so it may be. But while some people may be soothed by the probability that marriage will not become obsolete—in fact, that it may happen more often than ever—others, ourselves among them, are concerned about the kind of marriages people will have in the future. Coming together and then coming apart, no matter how many times the act is repeated, isn't a marriage. It may be little more than co-masturbation, which is the extent of many relationships that go by the name of marriage today. Inevitably, whenever it happens, divorce is a very painful experience. A rational person can hardly be ecstatic about that kind of a future.

If we resign ourselves to a future of serial, or successive, marriages, we are also resigning ourselves to a society in which men and women use each other coldly and selfishly as steps toward their individual maturity. Human beings grow, if they can grow at all, through their relationships with other human beings, but there is no justification for anyone maturing at the expense of another person. In all marriages the husband and wife begin with certain expectations; however wrong these expectations may be, the period of disenchantment and the final separation of the partners is a damaging experience. It may, in some cases, leave scars that make future relationships uncomfortable. Maturity at this price is a questionable commodity.

Another shadow over this kind of a future is the fact, only now becoming evident, that successive marriages don't work out well as frequently as we like to imagine. Recent magazine and newspaper stories have been playing up men and women whose second marriages have been more successful than their first, leading readers to assume that this is a trend. It isn't. It is true only of men and women who have managed to mature before marrying a second time, and these people are few in number. Figures being compiled on the survival rate of successive marriages are still incomplete, but in their preliminary stages they reveal what the trend actually is for most people: those who get divorced once are more likely to get divorced again. Apparently going through it once makes it easier the next time around—and perhaps the next.

It isn't likely that most men and women are going to

grow through marrying over and over. What is more plausible is that they are bound to leave a lot of hurt in their wake. We believe this isn't an inevitable characteristic of our future society.

What lies ahead?

Good marriages don't come apart, which is why the traditional wedding vows still have validity. Productive marriages grow and become more deeply satisfying to both partners. This is the kind of relationship we will need in a future that promises to be as kaleidoscopic as ours. Men and women who can fulfill their basic needs through a stable relationship with each other are far more adaptable as individuals, and adaptability will be the survival kit in the next age.

Our problem is that, as our society has been changing so rapidly, and as the pressures on the individual have increased, it has become harder for men and women to develop. This handicap makes it more difficult, often impossible, for many couples to achieve a good marriage.

It is important to realize that the marriages that are failing and the marriages that exist on the brink of deterioration are hardly marriages at all. These are relationships for which the marriage certificate accomplishes nothing. It cannot, for instance, provide commitment where there is a fear of being swallowed up; it cannot provide fidelity where there is a compulsion to be promiscuous; it cannot provide self-respect where there is self-contempt; nor can it provide adaptability to new influences where there is a death grip on fixed ideas.

These, unfortunately, are the kinds of marriages that threaten to overwhelm us in the future, *unless* we begin to accept the fact that:

a) Marriage is the intermeshing of adult human needs.
b) Men and women should get married *only* when they are mature.
c) While men and women are maturing, other forms of intimacy may be more suitable than marriage.

By "other forms of intimacy," we mean relationships such as free unions, communal memberships, or any of the various forms of living together without legal bonds. Those who want to avoid intimacy may even prefer the single life. We want to emphasize, however, that *these relationships are suggested as alternatives to marriage and not as substitutes.* They are not substitutes because they cannot offer a couple as much as marriage can. But they also do not make as many demands, and for this reason they impose less of a burden on a person who is trying to become a fully developed individual. These alternatives are nonbinding, so that as the growing person changes and begins to understand himself or herself more completely, he or she is not tied to a relationship formed to meet immature needs.

If you want a happy marriage . . .

There is no such thing as a "How-to Guide to a Happy Marriage." Many articles and books of bad advice go by such titles, and however well-intentioned their authors may have been, they frustrate their readers. No one can tell another person what he or she needs or how to get it. These books and articles only prescribe canned dialogue and pat, superficial answers to deeply felt, often unrealized, individual problems. They also encourage some husbands and wives to perpetuate marriages that really ought to be dissolved so that the partners might at least have a chance to find a better life, alone or with someone else.

In the following chapters, we will draw the line between good and bad marriages: what makes them happen, what holds them together, and, in the case of failing marriages, what tears them apart. Hopefully, by understanding how hidden forces can drive men and women into destructive, insecure relationships, the reader will realize how important it is for people to know their needs before committing themselves to a binding relationship with another person. By "needs" we mean the desires of the inner being. As long as there is a gap between those inner needs and the needs we display on the surface of our beings, a good marriage is impossible to achieve. It must wait for the person to outgrow his or her childish desires; otherwise the gap between what is real and what is imagined will be carried over into the marriage itself.

If you want a good marriage, you have to become a complete person. You have to find out who you are and what you need from another complete person. You also have to be able to perceive what the other person needs from you and be sure you're able to deliver. Until that time, and however long it may take, think before you marry.

3

How to Tell If You're Ready for Marriage

Are you ready to marry? The answer to that question has nothing to do with being old enough to get a marriage license. Are you mature enough to share a loving, productive, fulfilling, growing relationship with another person? Many men and women aren't, which is why marriages are failing at a higher rate than ever.

When you're burdened with inner conflicts, you don't really know what you want from life because you don't know who *you* are. This is evident in the comments of men and women whose marriages have come apart. So often they wonder what they ever saw in each other:

"I don't understand what happened to us, but I just don't love Bill any more. I can't help it. He's not the man I married."

"I've outgrown my wife. She can't give me what I need. She doesn't have it and never will. I wish I had seen that before we got married."

"I never thought George would be like this. He

was so devoted before we were married—I was the only girl in the world as far as he was concerned. Now he chases them all!"

Do marriages have to end like this? Does love always turn to resentment, or hatred, or simply not giving a damn? Must husbands and wives grow apart rather than together?

Will it happen to you? How can you be sure you're in love? And will that love last? How do you know you've found the person whose life you can share? Why would your marriage succeed when so many are failing? The answers to all these questions depend upon whether or not you and your prospective mate are ready for marriage. People who are well integrated come to marriage with the potential for maturity. After marriage, if they use their potential, they will continue to develop as individuals as well as developing as partners, but not in the erratic leaps and bounds of the emotional adolescent. They are flexible and can adapt to changes in their environment, in themselves, and in each other.

These people are able to see things as they are, not as they would like them to be. They aren't blinded by their hang-ups; neither are their infantile fantasies superimposed upon reality. Understanding who they are, they are much better equipped to understand others, especially the person whose life they choose to share. They can trust their feelings and communicate them to each other. Knowing that their desires come from deep within themselves, they can depend on them to last, to shape their lives.

But are *you* ready? That's the question you want to answer.

Unlike getting a driver's license, you can't take a performance test to find out whether you're ready for marriage. There just isn't any dry run for this unique experience, but you can ask yourself these questions before you marry:

1. *Are you in touch with your feelings?*

Your unconscious needs are determined by your entire life history and your unique personal characteristics. Understandably, they are your most potent desires. If they conflict with your conscious desires, there will be difficulties, because what you express consciously to yourself and others may not be what you really feel. If your conscious and unconscious needs harmonize, your deepest needs can rise to the surface of your life and be communicated.

Assuming that you are in touch with your inner feelings, how do you react to them? Can you accept your needs or are they repugnant to you?

If you're never satisfied, if you're continually disappointed with something once you succeed in getting it, or if people and situations always turn sour on you, it may be that you find your real needs repugnant. You may in fact cover them over with assumed needs that seem more acceptable but that you don't actually feel. Naturally, then, getting your imagined appetites fed will still leave you hungry for something else.

For example, do you have strong dependency needs and can you accept them? Are you looking for a mate you can lean on, someone who can give you a warm sense of security and take the lead in making the big decisions in life? Or does it bother you that you want to depend on someone? Does it make you appear weak and inadequate in your own eyes, and do you try to hide your real feelings by flaunting your independence? Do you fear your dependent needs so much that you won't even allow yourself to get close to anyone? And will you deliberately seek out a mate who must depend on you, just to prove to yourself that *you* don't really need anyone?

If you can accept your need to be dependent on your spouse, you'll probably marry a person who can give you the support you want. In fact, your spouse—provided he or she can also accept his or her inner needs—will probably be looking for someone just like you to do the leaning. If you both can gratify your other basic needs in this same give-and-take manner, you ought to have a good marriage.

But—if you're out of touch with your needs, you may choose someone who frustrates your inner needs because you cannot accept them. If you do, you'll be trying to share life with someone who is incapable of giving you the support you need. Don't forget, even though you can't face your needs, they do exist and they demand satisfaction. You'll end up blaming your mate because he or she continually lets you down, but until you are able to accept what you are, your relationships can't work out in any other way. If you can't accept yourself, how can anyone else?

While we're using a dependency need as an example here, you can apply the same approach to any other basic motivations, such as the need to mother or father, to be mothered or fathered, the need to be aggressive or passive, or whatever you find in yourself.

2. *Can you live with yourself?*
Can you make yourself happy? Can you take care of the needs that only you can fulfill? Can you be alone in

a room and enjoy your own company? Can you go after what you want in life? Can you enjoy your success? Can you accept your failures?

In short, can you live with yourself or are you seeking someone else to define your identity for you?

It is only when you feel able to make a meaningful life for yourself that you will be ready to build a new life with another adult. You're ready to share, not to grab. But if you're incomplete, if you feel that you can't possibly be happy until that certain someone comes along and makes your dreams come true, you're in for a nightmare of a marriage.

No one but you can fulfill your need to emerge as a person. A husband or a wife can satisfy your needs for love, intimacy, mutual support, and sharing, but he or she is not equipped to make you what you want to become as an individual.

If your desire for money and financial security leads you into a successful career, that's fine. If money means nothing to you, if you're more wrapped up in the creation of things than in the marketing of them—and if your material desires are also modest—that's fine, too. Either way, you're doing your own thing in the way you want to do it. You're fulfilling your individual needs, and that will make you a better marriage partner.

If you want a lot of material things, but don't have the confidence to get them for yourself, if you envy outstanding people, but don't think you could possibly achieve anything worthwhile, or if you blame others for holding you back, you may be thinking that your future mate will give you everything you can't give yourself. If you want to get away from your parents, but don't think you could live alone, you may see marriage as the answer to your problem. It isn't. Not having the experience of providing for your own needs, your demands on the capabilities of your mate will be outrageous. He or she will never be able to give you enough because your needs will be unrealistic. You may also attract a mate who unconsciously wants to fail, and you'll make sure that he or she does so —constantly. That's not a marriage, as you'll soon find out.

The so-called spoiled child often is handicapped by the kind of attention he gets from his parents. The sun rises and sets on him, he no sooner points to something than it becomes his, his achievements are exaggerated, his whims are indulged. Although such a person may have a natural desire to take care of himself, he doesn't know how. Emotionally he is a child, no matter what his chronological age, and if he marries before he grows up, his mate will never be able to satisfy him. In the first place he won't really know what he wants because he isn't in touch with himself; and then, being a child, his desires may change radically from moment to moment. If this describes you, or the person you want to marry, look into yourself before going to the altar.

When you get married, you don't dump yourself in someone's lap and say, "Well, here I am—make me happy!" People often expect this to happen, and of course they're wrong. What they should be doing is saying those words to themselves—long before they get married. Then, when they do marry, they can be responsible for themselves and can seek their individual goals. They'll be ready to contribute all they have to give to a whole new experience with another person.

If you're satisfied with your life, if you enjoy what you're doing, and if you feel you're going in a direction that's right for you, then you're assuming responsibility for your needs. You're learning what you can and can't do, you're discovering your own values, and you're living by them.

3. *Can you communicate your needs?*

Do people know what you really want? Or are you constantly asking for one thing but wanting another? Worse than that, are you one of those vague people who can only criticize what you get and never be specific about what you want?

If you're not in touch with your feelings, you can't very well communicate them. But if you do know what you need from people, you have to let them know it too. This is especially important when it comes to the person you want to marry. Perceptive and sensitive as he or she may be, you can't expect your future mate to guess what you want without a little help from you.

You and the person you want to marry have to know what you can expect from each other. It's a mistake to think that once you're married you'll be able to "work things out." That's too much of a risk to take. How do you know your spouse will be able to give you what you need? How does he or she know you can satisfy a partner? Now, not later, is the time to find out.

People who can accept themselves as they really are don't have to camouflage their desires. They can express them freely, without apologies. They know that since their needs are reasonable, they can expect them to be fulfilled.

Today we hear a lot about the lack of communication between husbands and wives. While this is often true, it's important to realize that communication involves far more than an exchange of words. People communicate in many ways—by physical gestures, facial expressions, tone of voice, but above all by their moods and feelings, many of which they never put into words. When we talk about the "vibrations" we feel, that's what we mean, for these emotions are transmitted from person to person as surely as if they were shouted in so many words. This is especially true of married persons.

Many husbands and wives "walk on eggs" when it comes to communicating their feelings. Because they are uncomfortable with their own needs and emotions, and perhaps believe there is something wrong with them, they're afraid to bring them out in the open. They hedge when it comes to discussing some of the important issues between them and their partner. They're afraid that if they admit their inner feelings they will arouse their partner's anger. Consequently the emotions they communicate most clearly to each other are fear, anxiety, and dishonesty. The relationship then becomes a game of hide-and-seek, with neither partner able to locate or communicate with his authentic mate. In that sense it is a nonrelationship.

Are there some touchy subjects that you'd rather not discuss with your prospective marriage partner? Are you afraid to talk about your real needs? Can you be open about whether or not you want children, how much money you need to feel comfortable, how important your career is to you, whether you want to continue your education? Are you, as a woman, afraid to admit that you want to return to work or to school after you're married, or after your children are old enough to attend school? Are you, as a man, reluctant to express what you want in your marriage? Can you and your prospective mate discuss these issues, or do your attempts end in confrontations, nit-picking, and destructive criticism?

In a marriage, it is important for the partners to be able to talk about anything, openly and without apology.

When a couple can discuss their feelings freely, the air is often cleared and the two can be brought closer together by a better understanding of themselves and each other. In this way the marriage grows through the mutual concern of each partner for the other. For instance, if their feelings conflict, their differences can lead them to thoughtful self-examination. There doesn't have to be a power play in which each partner clings to a rigid position to prove he or she can withstand the attacks of the other. Instead, one partner will usually realize that he or she can give way without any loss of self-esteem and can thereby help the other partner to grow.

4. *Can you face your problems instead of blaming them on somebody else?*

Do you wish you could attract a man who is strong and successful instead of the losers you always seem to meet? Do you wish that, just for once, you could find a woman who isn't out to take everything you've got? Does your boss use you for a doormat? Do your friends always borrow things and never give them back? Do men love you and leave you? Do women always mother you? If patterns such as these appear repeatedly in your life, it's unlikely that everyone is out to do you wrong. Rather, it's possible that *you're* the one who's causing the trouble. You might be *making* people behave the way they do so that you can blame them for your hang-ups.

Here are two common examples: If you're a man whose mother used to smother you with attention one minute and then withdraw it when you weren't a "good boy," you may think all women are takers. Naturally, you don't enjoy feeling that way, so you are apt to cover it up by telling yourself (and everyone else) that you're crazy about women. Your actions speak differently, however, because that inner resentment is still there. Because the pressure from it makes you uncomfortable, you want to blame someone for it, which of course you're likely to do. It's easy, too, especially if you make a point of going out with women who are just like your mother. The others will only prove that your whole attitude is wrong, whereas you want to be right. Much as you don't want to dislike women, you're trying to justify your prejudice.

If you're a man-hating woman, it may be that you had a cold, detached father who made you think that all men were like him. The trouble is, you'll try to disguise that conviction at the same time you're trying to prove how right it is. You'll keep affectionate men at a distance and go after the cold fish. Then you'll be able to tell yourself, "Men have no feelings at all. No wonder they make me dislike them!"

While all of us, in one way or another, have problems, many find it very difficult to focus on them; and when we do, it's often easier to blame someone or something else. This usually gets us nowhere. It's important that we try to "own" our problems if we can. If you find yourself behaving irrationally, and if the same "bad breaks" keep coming your way, you can begin to look inside yourself for the cause. Perhaps you can find it yourself, but if you can't, you would do well to seek help.

Influenced by the women's movement, some women are blaming men for their hang-ups. Not everyone of these accusations is deserved. Very often a woman is held back only because she hasn't prepared herself to move ahead. In any rap session you can find wives blaming husbands for holding them back and confining them to a life of boredom and drudgery. As some of them see it, they could have had an interesting job out in the world where everything is happening; they could be meeting fascinating people, finding out what's going on, improving their minds, becoming better persons, using their talents, making some money, living a little . . . if *only* the men in their lives hadn't stopped them. But if someone suggests that some of these women go after those things right now, that they equip themselves to satisfy their needs to be independent by completing their training for whatever they want to do, or by going out and getting a job that interests them, they always seem to find an excuse to remain overly dependent, passive, and frustrated. These are the women who can't face their own problems, and as long as they can blame men, they won't do anything to resolve them.

Are you one of these women? Or are you able to enjoy a woman's expanded opportunities? Are you ready to take on the responsibilities as well as the rewards of an independent life? Are you also aware that you may occasionally be tripped up by your former attitudes, and that you may try to duck such things as making big decisions or taking the consequences of your actions? Perhaps, when you're in a spot, you revert to behaving like a little girl in order to get out of it. Are you aware of these lapses when they occur, and can you be good-natured about them? Most important, can you admit them and try to nip them in the bud next time they appear?

And what about the men who are affected by the new woman? They're having problems, too, some of which they're blaming on women. The old-fashioned male chauvinist blames the new woman for every problem under the sun, from drug pushing to the high price of food. This gives him an excuse to vent the hostility he has always felt toward women. Some men who are insecure in other areas are so overwhelmed by the prospect of female independence that they join it rather than fight it. They become the most outspoken champions of the liberation movement, blaming themselves and other men more bitterly than any woman could. These men, too, are looking for scapegoats for their problems.

Are you one of these men who find women such a convenient target for blame? Do they threaten your security? Or are you mature enough to encourage women to develop themselves as persons, to welcome them as full partners in life, and to appreciate their individual contributions to society—whether they choose to work at home or in the arts, the professions or the business world? Do you have enough confidence in yourself that you can applaud someone else's achievements? Would you rather look a woman in the eye than look down at her? Do you sometimes find yourself treating a woman as if she were a little girl. When you do, can you laugh at yourself and acknowledge the distortion as your own?

5. *Can you see your future mate as he or she really is? Or are you seeing things that aren't there?*

Can this man or woman give you what you need? Or are you imagining things? Do you need something so desperately that you can't see straight?

For example, do you want to become Cinderella so badly that you think your man is Prince Charming when he's actually the Joker? Does your need for affection trick you into mistaking good manners for kindness and consideration?

No husband or wife should be expected to give a person what he or she didn't get from parents. Yet this is how some men and women deceive themselves into marrying the wrong mate. They expect a mate to give them not only what they need now but whatever they have missed in life. Of course it never happens. Nevertheless, the poor mate is blamed for letting the spouse down, when actually he or she never had the capacity to satisfy such needs.

If you didn't get your fair share of love, respect, and affection in your earlier years, it's a loss you'll have to live with. No one can ever make it up to you, but if you keep insisting that someone should, you may ruin the rest of your life—and someone else's—by looking for something that doesn't exist.

So if you find that you frequently have to give your future mate the benefit of the doubt before your marriage, if you keep telling yourself that he or she "really isn't like that, not deep down inside," you have good reason to suspect that your vision is blurred by an irrational need.

How do you know whether you can see straight? That depends upon how well you know yourself. If you are in touch with your feelings, then you know what is going on inside you. And, being aware of your needs—for instance, knowing that your position as the youngest child in a very large family may make you overeager for attention—you won't allow them to distort your perception. You'll pay much more attention to your realistic needs to love and be loved as a whole person.

6. *Can you really share?*

If you can take care of your needs, fine. But do you try to act so independent that you can't share your life with someone else? If you never need anybody, then you may need help.

You can't satisfy all your needs. You can't give yourself a feeling of belonging and of being loved, and you can't experience intimacy by yourself. There has to be another person in your life, or else these needs to share will remain frustrated.

Today there's a lot of talk about marriages that allow the couples to go their separate ways. If he doesn't like concerts, she goes alone or with friends; if she's too tired to go to a party after working all day, he goes by himself; they take separate vacations; they have separate and often contrary social activities; sometimes they have separate sex lives. There is good reason to suspect that these couples are unable to achieve a shared experience. This is especially true of marriages where both partners have sexual problems. Very often the root of their inability to have successful intercourse with each other is a basic fear of the other. She's afraid of men (or of her ability to hold a man) and he's afraid of women (because he thinks they'll reject him).

It's important to look at your other relationships in life. For instance, how do you feel about your friends? Can you do a friend a favor without feeling superior about it? Can you ask for a favor without feeling inferior? Do you keep your friends at a distance, or are you a part of their lives?

How do you feel about your future partner? Is he or she adding something to your life? Are you adding to his or her life? Can you enjoy new experiences together? Can you accept his or her point of view?

If you feel threatened by another person's presence in your life, if you feel you can't belong to someone without losing your identity as an individual, if sex presents you with a choice of being swallowed up or demolished, you have problems that ought to be solved before you attempt to share your life with another person.

Loving and being loved enhances, even strengthens, your sense of being an individual, because it is for your unique qualities as a person that you are loved. You're not being asked to change or to submerge yourself in another personality; you're being asked to share what you are, and in return to share what your mate is. Your life together should reflect both your personalities. And because you are mature, the prospect of a shared sexual relationship with your partner offers you erotic stimulation that can be satisfied in the most delightful ways.

Many men and women are misled by people who can't share and who may be trying to find acceptance for their way of nonmarriage. You can have the same experiences in a dormitory without going to all the bother of a wedding—and very likely a divorce.

7. *Are you aware of the influence your parents may have had on you and your expectations?*

A mature person looks at life through his or her own eyes, not through the eyes of his or her parents. Your parents had reasons for their hang-ups, but you may simply be carrying on the symptoms without a reason of your own. Nevertheless, unless you can distinguish between your problems and those of your parents, you may be letting your parents' problems interfere with your life.

If there was a serious illness in your family when you were a child, you may still suffer some emotional effects from it. For instance, a woman whose mother was confined to a hospital or a mental institution when she was very young may resent men. She may have blamed her father for sending her mother away. To the child's eyes it may have seemed that he had an awesome power over her mother—and consequently over women in general. Thus she may feel that men are overwhelming, and to defend herself she may try to "cut them down to size."

Or perhaps she expects too much of men, so that, in her eyes, they continually fail to please her.

A person's early experiences can affect his later relationships in many ways. For instance, it's not unusual for a man whose father died when he was very young to fear being rejected. To a young boy the death of a parent means the withdrawal of that parent's love, which is a particularly painful feeling of abandonment to an adolescent. Such a man, if he has been hurt by this kind of a shock, will find it difficult to believe he is loved. He'll keep testing and testing a woman, always expecting her to throw him over, until finally she may very well do just that.

8. *How do you know you want to get married?*

People get married for all kinds of reasons. Some want to get away from their parents and are unable to do it on their own. Some are pressured into marriage by their families. Some are afraid that if they don't get married it means they are homosexual.

On the other side of the picture, when two people fall in love and really care for each other, they want to be together most of the time. They want to share themselves and their lives with each other. Of course, they have to be able to bend to each other's needs, but not to the point where they lose their own identity. This preservation of identity is something they respect in each other, so that neither feels something must be sacrificed in coming together. Rather, as they encourage and help each other to grow and realize their individual goals, they should feel they have gained something through the marriage.

Unless there is this desire to share, to bend and to

participate in another person's life, relationships other than marriage might be more comfortable.

Becoming aware of life-shaping relationships and events in your past is an important step toward your development as an individual. It means that your hang-ups can no longer distort your present and future relationships and behavior. In other words, you can begin to look at life through "now" eyes rather than those of yesterday.

Awareness, however, is not enough. The events and the persons in your past life cannot be changed or erased. They happened and they must be accepted before you can be free of their hold on you. For instance, by accepting your parents as they really were and are, with all their faults as well as their virtues, you can then go on to become what you are. But if you can't accept others, you'll never be able to accept yourself. If you can't get close to yourself, you'll never get close to your future marriage partner.

Questioning yourself may require some hard answers. If you've been honest with yourself, you may not like some of the things you've learned about yourself. But how much better it is to learn them now, before you complicate your life and someone else's with a marriage that doesn't work. You can also take a step toward maturity by acknowledging what you are and by giving yourself the time and opportunity to grow out of your immaturity into a whole person. Some of us need more time than others.

PART
II

IS MARRIAGE
OBSOLETE?

4

Living Together in a World That's Coming Apart

A New York psychotherapist was listening to a young couple who were consulting him for the first time. They had been living together for six months, they told him, but lately they had begun to feel uneasy about their relationship. Something that used to be there was gone. "Maybe we ought to get married," the young man suggested, obviously expecting the psychotherapist to make a decision for him.

The psychotherapist smiled. "Why?" he said, throwing his arms out wide. "Why spoil a good love affair?"

The young couple were startled and disappointed. They had hoped for a stereotyped answer that would relieve them of a responsibility they couldn't handle.

When the young man and woman were first attracted to each other, they expressed their contempt for marriage. Both came from homes broken by divorce and remarriage, and they were reluctant to commit themselves to a relationship that might end in the same way. In their eyes, marriage stifled love. But their feeling for each other was changing. At times they couldn't communicate as freely as they once did. The young woman was particularly uncomfortable because the young man was becoming possessive. He didn't like her friends, he was jealous of the men with whom she worked, and he objected when her job required her to work during the hours he was free. He complained that she was always trying to make him jealous by flirting with other men. He didn't like her friends, he said, because she deliberately picked them to make him appear inadequate by comparison.

This couple clearly was not ready to get married. In fact, they were growing apart because the young woman was maturing faster than the young man. He, sensing that he was losing her, was trying to hold onto her by means of marriage. She was afraid to end the relationship because it made her think she was following in her mother's footsteps and unable to hold onto a man. Marriage seemed to offer her permanency. Had these two people married, both would have been miserable because the disparity in their emotional ages would have made it impossible for either of them to satisfy the other.

The psychotherapist was saying, "Better to have a broken love affair than a broken marriage." And he was right.

Today many young people are afraid of marriage, and for good reasons. Like the couple above, they have seen the wreckage of broken homes from the inside. Some of them have grown up in unhappy homes held together "for the children's sake," and they know what an agonizing experience that can be. Unfortunately, bad marriages are the only example of marriage many young people have seen, and it's understandable that they blame the institution rather than the individuals who enter it.

A fear of marriage, however, doesn't make people any wiser about it. It simply means that they try to avoid marriage until other pressures force them into it. These pressures come, not from the church or society, but often from past experiences and conflicts in the life histories of the partners. Marriage becomes an illusory way to satisfy the infantile demands or to cover them up—often both at the same time.

Not all young people are afraid of marriage. Some are slow to approach it because they realize that they do not yet know what they need to make them happy. For example, a young man and woman, both of them twenty-two years old, have been living together for almost a year, and they think that eventually they may get married. But not now. They're an unusual couple in that both are finding success early in their careers. He's a commercial illustrator and she's a singer, and they give a lot of themselves to their work. "We're not old enough to get married," she says, "and we know it."

Both these people have had the advantages of success, money, travel, contact with interesting people, *and* a happy family background. But they're aware that they appear to be more ready for marriage than they really are. "So much is happening to us—we need time to catch up on the inside," the young man has said. On the deeper levels of their beings they are unsure of who and what they are, and for this reason they shy away from taking on the responsibilities of a committed relationship.

There *are* exceptions among young people today. Some couples marry early and make a go of it. They seem to know what they can expect from themselves, and they seek mates who can give them what they need.

For example, a young midwestern couple has taken a

more realistic approach to their educational needs than the couple described in the first chapter. She was able to finish college before he did because he spent a few years in the army. Now she's started on a career that gives her a chance to use her training and talents and also pays her a good salary. The couple is able to live quite well while he attends school full time, working toward an advanced degree. They aren't planning on a family right now, but, as she says, "In a few years we'll really enjoy having children." Her husband's career will be well on its way and she will have gained enough experience in hers to enable her to return to it, if she chooses, when their children are older.

This husband and wife respect each other's goals, and in helping each other to achieve them they are actually creating one new life out of their two separate ones. They don't compete with each other; they complement each other. He, for instance, is proud that his wife has a good job, and she's happy that her husband is going after a career that means something to him. "Some people think of us as 'making sacrifices,' " he has said, "but the way we look at it, we're taking advantage of our opportunities."

The maturity of this couple is uncommon today. So is the awareness of the couple who realize that they are not ready for marriage. The first couple, unfortunately, is far more typical of most people who marry. They are unsure of themselves, blind to their real needs, and dependent upon external labels and accessories for their identity. In another age, perhaps in a culture more stable than ours, they might have been able to hide their uncertainties behind a marriage, provided their partners didn't make too many demands on them. Today this is not possible. We live in a different kind of society, one that puts far more pressures on people. Our world makes growing up more difficult at the same time that it shows no mercy to those who can't keep pace.

Some men and women have a way of making marriage look like a good thing. And so it is—for them. They are able to meet its demands. They are able to adjust to another human being without giving up their own identity. They can integrate their needs with those of another person. What they feel, they can express. They can communicate love. In other words, they are aware of their identity. They can influence their environment.

For other couples, marriage has become a bad trip. They can't accept their own needs in life, much less those of another person, and they cannot adjust to something new. Every change in their environment threatens to destroy the personality they have assumed to cover up their insecurities. They can't express what they want because they don't know what that is, which also means that they can't be satisfied. They behave in ways they don't understand because they are unaware of the needs that drive them. They aren't aware of themselves as a force in life; instead, they realize only that they react, erratically and unpredictably, to their surroundings. They are, in fact, its victims.

The Age of Unfeel

The undeveloped person has been defending himself against the changes in our culture by cutting himself off completely from his feelings. Because his inner tumult is more than he can tolerate, he denies that it exists. But in so doing he denies that he himself exists. Without his feelings, all he has left is the role he has assumed, which is merely a phantom. The phantom has no contact with his inner desires and cannot express the person he is. He cannot leave his mark on life. He is easily altered by every fad, every change in our style of living. It is like a suit of clothes that may suddenly go out of style, leaving the wearer bare. This is a neurosis born of our culture.

In the recent past, psychotherapists noted that their patients were suffering from the repression of their behavior and the inhibition of their emotions. Now they are reporting a new trend: Today their patients are suffering from the effects of inadequate control.

Ideally, man's actions should flow from his inner feelings. Feelings and actions should be integrated in such a way that the individual has the freedom to choose when to act and when not to act. It's as erroneous to say that all feelings should be inhibited as it is to say that they all should be acted upon. In either case, the individual must be responsible for the results of what he does; and those results may be helpful, destructive, or anything in between. Here is where a person makes a decision—not a *judgment*—to do or not to do. He must weigh the value of inhibiting an emotional need against the results of acting it out. This is freedom of choice. People must make new decisions constantly, even where the same emotion is involved, because what might be considered destructive behavior in one situation may not be so in another. An emotion, quite innocent in itself, cannot be categorized for all time.

Changing a personality takes a long time, and human beings are impatient. Relatively few are willing to go through the process of unraveling the tangled threads of their beings, sorting out their real identity from the one they have been using as a façade. A short cut was what more and more people began to demand, and now they have come up with one.

In our world, many people detach themselves, paying no attention to their feelings at all, in the mistaken belief that this is an easier way to deal with them. But by cutting themselves off from their emotions they have complicated their problems. Now they cannot feel; now they are locked into the world and out of themselves, and rather than being liberated they have become the prisoners of their environment. They do what they assume society expects of them; they feel—or *try* to feel—what they think is appropriate to their image.

Here's how the pattern works: Instead of feeling, first, they act first and then *hope* to feel something. But nothing happens. That's why we hear the words *empty* and *meaningless* so often these days. If the feeling doesn't come first, there can be no sensation of fulfillment.

For example, many people are talking about peace and love today, but there is a big difference between talking about a feeling and experiencing it within yourself. Acting out the pantomime of love doesn't make a person loving. This is trying to feel an emotion merely by going through the gestures associated with it.

We are human beings, not angels. We can only begin to talk about peace and love when we are able to accept the fact that they coexist with all our other human responses to life—and they include such feelings as hate and resentment along with love and good will.

Sexually, a great many people are also suffering from an absence of feeling. In the belief that sex—by itself and for its own sake—is "good" for them, many are going through the motions of the sex act and wondering why they aren't getting anything out of it. They're asking why they don't *feel* anything. But if people don't experience sexual desire, how can they know satisfaction? If they deny their need for closeness and intimacy, how can they experience the pleasures of a shared life?

By trying to escape from himself, many a modern man has become a detached, empty, and lonely creature. He is afraid to trust. He cannot get close to anyone for fear that his real self will be detected, a prospect he considers unacceptable, even loathesome. His inner being is so full of pain that he wants to avoid the slightest bruise from anything on the outside. He seeks easy answers to deep questions, magical solutions to hypercomplex problems. He just wants to stay cool.

And yet he dimly senses the loss of his distinctly human qualities—his ability to think, to organize facts, to gain insights into situations, to create, to interact with other human beings, and especially to be conscious of his feelings and aware of his existence. Because he cannot exert his influence on the dehumanizing effects of our environment, because he allows himself to function like one of its mechanical parts, he feels more like a light bulb that glows at the press of a button.

In a pitiful attempt to reestablish contact with their feelings, some people have freaked out with drugs. Some are "trying" the new therapies that claim to be able to put people back in touch with their emotions. Some are taking a hedonistic route in an attempt to experience pleasure—any kind, right here and right now. But even these so-called cures usually turn out to be another way of avoiding a confrontation with the real self. Instead, these individuals keep trying to acquire the feelings of their assumed role—and in our fast-changing world that role is destined for a short life.

What's in a word?

As people change, as different needs become more important than others, as society exerts new pressures on human life-styles, marriage also changes. More mature people can accept this. Because of their flexibility, they can bend to meet new situations. Less mature people cannot. They depend upon rigid definitions of their roles, and when those definitions are changed, they feel as if their identity is being assaulted. They cling to relationships and situations as they were, refusing to face what they really have become. Consequently life often fails to live up to their expectations. This is especially evident in their marriages.

To the person who defines marriage as a legal union of a man and a woman who agree to live together permanently, the realities of married life are full of contradictions. Marriage is not always permanent, as the divorce figures indicate. With both men and women involved in activities that may take them away from home for long periods of time, we can't even say that husbands and wives are people who live together on a daily basis.

And what of the partners themselves? Today who can define "husband" and "wife"? If anything, we are moving away from definitions because we realize that it is more important for people to be themselves than to act out roles.

The alienated husband

In the past it was easier for men and women to take on the roles of husband and wife because these roles were clearly defined along distinct sexual lines. Men *did* certain things, women *did* others.

Usually a man's work called for the use of his muscles and strength, so it was easier for a man to identify with what he did. Women couldn't do that work. And as well as a man performed his work, he could always try to do better, because what he did for a living reflected what he was as a man. It was also a "man's job" to support his family and provide for all its basic needs. No one ever asked whether a man was ready for so much responsibility; it was simply assumed that, being a man, he was. If he needed any examples, he could look to his father and grandfather, whose roles were very much the same as his.

Now, however, we are living in a technological world where work has little or no sexual connotation. We cannot identify ourselves as men or women through what we do for a living. Very often a job is hardly more than a repetition of motions that men and women can learn to do equally well. In large businesses, most of the employees may not even realize how their work relates to the organization's function as a whole. Who can find any identity in that?

The alienated man is the one who is more likely to be working not at what he really wants to do—because his desires are not permitted to motivate him—but rather at dull, tedious jobs that enable him to go through the motions of being an adult. He is the one who complains that jobs have become so standardized that his work gives him no opportunity to feel that he is a man. He does his job not for fulfillment but for the paycheck. He has no pride in his work, because it has no meaning for him. Nor does he try to increase his productivity, because it seems that no one will know, no one will care, and no one will reward him for it. Instead he looks forward to a shorter work week and a longer lunch hour. He blames the "system" for not making better use of him, but he lacks the ego-strength to make a change in his way of life. Afraid to get out and test himself in the marketplace because he fears he will be overcome by stronger men, he settles for tenure and fringe benefits.

Because the insecure man cannot take responsibility for his own needs, he resents the additional burden of his family's needs. He plays the part of a breadwinner, but he does it grudgingly. Instead of trying to find a solution to his inner sense of frustration, he seeks to escape from its discomfort. He comes home at night to forget himself in too many drinks; he spends his weekends on the golf course, away from the demands of his family; as often as he can, he gets together with "the boys," taking nostalgic memory trips back to high school and college days when he had no responsibilities. He tries to prove that he's still a man through sexual experiences, in and out of marriage.

The "liberated" wife

Not all women are liberated. Relatively few are able to take advantage of their broader opportunities, and many lack the security to break out of the mold in which they have been cast for so many generations. This is especially true of middle-aged women. These women often are confused by the prospect of freedom from tradition. They feel more secure in clearly designated roles of woman, wife, and mother because there they can take on a ready-made identity. But as these roles are disintegrating they are leaving many women on shaky ground.

The woman who has been brought up to believe that her place is in the home may feel guilty when she leaves it for a job. Even though she may arrange to have her home kept clean, her children responsibly supervised, and family meals served at the proper time, she may be uneasy about abandoning the role that labeled her a woman. Holding down a job, however interesting it may be, may convince her that she is more aggressive than a woman ought to be. And if her husband is also unsure of himself to the point where he resents his wife's capabilities outside the home, she may begin to wonder whether she is a woman at all. On the other hand, if she stays at home to take care of the house, mind the children and see to her husband's needs, she may feel that she is not living up to the liberated concept of a woman. Either way, she is frustrated because she is not able to shape her life according to her own inner needs.

If a twentieth-century wife has an image of a husband as a man who comes home to dinner every night, mows the lawn on weekends, fixes everything that breaks down, and earns enough money to provide for all the family needs, she will be thoroughly confused by the realities of her life. If her husband's business requires him to miss some of her home-cooked meals or to travel frequently, she may accuse him of failing to live up to his responsibilities as a man. If he is so busy working that he must hire someone to mow the lawn, or if he must leave some of the traditional "male" chores to his wife, she may resent being burdened with tasks she never expected to do. Being inflexible, she cannot adapt herself to new ways.

The inflexible wife is the one who complains that she's bored, neglected, repressed, unloved, and left to play both father and mother to her children. When she finishes cleaning the house—and this is work she finds repetitious and menial—she finds nothing to do. She resists any efforts to get her involved in continuing her education, participating in community projects, or developing her skills because, she says, she's too busy being a chauffeur to her kids. Envious of women who have both a career and a family life, she blames her husband for depriving her of her opportunities to do the same. Little does she realize that she has never prepared herself for a more interesting existence.

If a woman is hung up on the old-fashioned idea that the man is the family's sole source of income, she may resent having to go out and get a job to help finance her children's education. She may not be able to understand that very few men can earn enough money to meet a family's basic needs in a society with such a high standard of living. Instead she may regard her husband as a failure simply because she must now assume some of the responsibilities that "should be" his. Because he is not living up to his traditional role, she cannot live up to hers, and to this kind of woman this is disturbing.

Husbands and wives who are caught in the gap between what they expected marriage to be and what it really is are unable to help each other. Frightened by the changes that are coming into their lives against their will, they can only try to ward off reality. They blame each other for their disillusionment. They play on each other's weaknesses and aim their hostility where it can cause the most pain. They confirm and reinforce each other's sense of failure, the wife telling the husband that he is not a man and he accusing her of not being a woman. Beneath the deteriorating façade of each is a frustrated, unhappy child who is threatened with exposure.

If a husband's need is more for a mother than a mate, he may feel abandoned by a wife who attempts to develop a career outside the home. He may feel inadequate if she simply gets a job to help pay their bills. He may indulge himself in fantasies about her involvement with other men—men to whom he feels inferior because he can't fit into his unrealistic image of what a husband should be. He may feel that his wife is competing with him to get a better job or to earn more money. He may feel neglected, misunderstood, unloved because his wife has other interests in her life. He may seek his mothering from other women.·

The wife who wants a father more than a husband may feel cheated by a man who turns over some of "his" responsibilities to her. If her husband believes it is more convenient for her to pay the bills and balance the checkbook, she may interpret it as a sign of his inability to behave like a man. If she is left alone at home while her husband flies to places she imagines as glamorous and exciting, she too may feel neglected and abandoned. If, on the other hand, he agrees that she would be happier working at a career that would challenge her abilities, she may feel disappointed because he is not exercising a paternal authority over her. She may even attempt to find a father in another man.

While these are only a few of the complications that can disrupt the relationship of a husband and wife, they illustrate the kind of pressures our way of life exerts on marriage. It's not surprising that our divorce rate continues to soar.

The rebellious offspring

The presence of children often intensifies a disturbed relationship between a husband and wife. Insecure parents may resent the attention given to a child, or perhaps they may try to relive their own childhood through their offspring. Inevitably the child is influenced and, in many cases, handicapped by the frustrations of the parents. This is evident in our present youth generation.

While there has been much talk about the gap between the generations, not enough attention has been paid to the thread of continuity running between them. In their outspokenness, in their rejection of materialistic goals, in their contempt for an overly aggressive way of life, the younger generation is said to be rebelling *against* its parents. What we have overlooked is their rebellion in behalf of their parents.

Many of today's young people were born to immature parents who thought that material success was the badge of the adult. Their goal in life was to make money and get security, and they settled for whatever they could get after that. They became the first American generation that went to college en masse, many of them after losing years of their youth to a war. After college there was a career to be made, a family to raise, a house with a mortgage to be paid, and children to educate, all of which reinforced their image. To accomplish these goals the parent generation demonstrated a tremendous amount of self-discipline and dedication. They also made sacrifices, the most costly being the satisfaction of their inner desires. While these men and women chose to do the things that suited the roles they were playing, their hunger for other things was communicated—unconsciously—to their children.

The parent generation that conformed to the life-style promoted by the corporate world is the same one criticized for being too permissive with its children. The couples who lived side by side in identical houses on duplicated streets encouraged their children to think in highly individual ways. Now the son or daughter who wants to do his or her thing (and not necessarily make a lot of money out of it) may be living out the supressed wishes of a parent who put his own needs aside. The father who complains loudly that his son's hair is too long and his clothes are a mess may unconsciously applaud him for thumbing his nose at social conventions. And yet, such a son may be fettered, because in his very rebellion he is carrying out his father's unconscious wishes when he should be attending to his own needs.

A similar thread is evident between many immature mothers and their daughters, although here we find more attention given to the new sexual freedom among women. Men have always had more sexual privileges, but only recently have women been able to claim them for themselves. Modern contraceptives that are cheap, easy to take, and accessible now allow women to experience sex as something apart from procreation. For some women, however, this opportunity has come too late.

These mothers are often both envious of and disturbed by their daughters' sexual attitudes. Some were women who preserved their virginity until marriage. Whether they did it through fear of an unwanted pregnancy or through obedience to an upbringing that put a premium on chastity, it no longer matters. Today, who cares! What does matter is that these women, seeing their daughters enjoying sexual relationships that appear to be free of fears or guilt, resent having missed out on the experience.

To women who married *because* they were pregnant, the current social tolerance of free love is bound to be tormenting. Many of these women, forced into marriage for the wrong reasons and often with the wrong mate, feel that they paid an unfair price for something that is no longer considered a crime.

Like many fathers of young men, these mothers unconsciously communicated their desires to their daughters, inspiring in them a strong contempt for the restrictions on their parents' way of life. As they see it, their daughters can experiment with sex without being trapped into a permanent relationship with a man they do not love. They can put off marriage as long as they choose, and in the meantime they can have a career, meet different men, travel, drive their own cars, live in their own apartments—in short, they can do all the glamorous things their mothers feel they have missed in their lives. The question that has yet to be answered is, Are these young women living out their own desires or those of their mothers?

A family comes full circle

Ironically, the youth generation, whose ideals have been so influenced by their parents, is now having an effect upon the lives of its parents. No longer do little boys and girls dress up like their fathers and mothers; now it's the fathers who copy their sons' casual clothes and the mothers who wear jeans.

Seeing their children living out the desires they never could indulge, many parents are becoming dissatisfied with their ways of life. The disappointment and frustration that many wives and husbands have experienced are rising to the surface, and many marriages that held together for years are coming apart. Very often neither partner can identify the source of his unhappiness. Because of these confused feelings, these couples can only blame each other for their failures and hope that they can get something better out of a fresh start.

The dissolution of marriages "after the children are grown" has unfortunate effects on many of the young. They may feel that the family life they have known was a hoax. Marriage, like many of their parents' other relationships or values, may seem to be one more thing that they ought to reject.

The "mature" experience

It would be misleading to imply that the pressures in our culture are felt only by those who are insecure. This is not so. Almost all men and women find our society a very difficult one in which to live. In today's world, people are faced with a changing environment, which often means that they must find new ways to gratify their inner needs. The difference is that more mature people can adapt to their surroundings. Knowing what they require from them, they can be more selective.

Through their freedom of choice, these men and women put the stamp of their own identity on their environment. They reject what is useless. They do the things that mean something to them rather than "what everyone else is doing." They do work that challenges them and leaves them satisfied rather than bored. Because they know what they enjoy, they usually find their jobs more interesting.

These men and women do not need labels for their

identity. Jobs don't have to connote sex differences, because these men and women know who they are. Their identity comes from within—they confront their own needs inside themselves.

In marriage they do not come together as actors playing roles. They are more genuine persons building a new life together, respecting each other's goals and helping each other to achieve them. Realizing that marriage is a major responsibility to take on, they are more willing to share the burden with each other. What does it matter who does which chores, as long as the responsibilities are met? Because their marriage reflects the personality of each partner, each contributes to its success. Each helps to ease the financial pressures on their marriage. Each shares in the upbringing of their children if they choose to become parents. And each sees to it that the basic needs of husband and wife are satisfied.

In our complex society, more than in any other, marriage is a relationship for adults. Unfortunately, the enormous pressures on the development of a human being, from the moment he is born, make it more difficult to mature. Before we can fully understand the dilemma of the immature person in our culture, we have to know how he got to be the way he is.

5

Who Isn't Ready for Marriage

When a man and a woman get married, no matter how well they may think they know each other, they come together as strangers. Perhaps they lived together before they got married, or perhaps they went together from the time they were two. Perhaps they can tell what the other is thinking by a look in the eyes, and they may know each other's favorite foods and just where the sore spots are. But they *still* don't know each other. How can they? They are bringing two totally distinct living histories together into one new way of life. And in this case it's what they don't know that *can* hurt them!

When a man and a woman live together without a legal commitment, their feelings for each other may be very strong, but they also are free to go their own way whenever they please. They have no responsibility for each other, nor do they need any mutual goals.

In the security of a legal commitment, a man and a woman gradually reveal more of what they are because there is less fear of rejection and abandonment. They have the time and the relaxed environment in which to know and be known. They see each other through the good and the bad times, realizing that a crisis or a problem will not necessarily shatter their relationship. If they can satisfy each other's innermost needs, if they can help each other attain their individual goals, and if they can work together toward their mutual goals, these two strangers will become loving friends. If, in their familiarity, they frustrate each other, crippling their abilities and undermining their self-confidence, they will become each other's enemy.

If two relatively mature people get married, they are likely to be more ready to meet the demands of living together. They are able to give and receive love, and they are willing to share an intimate existence with each other. Together they can plan and build their life; they can enjoy each other's sexuality, and in time they may give new life to the world. Together they will struggle to make a living, to hold onto a home and, if they have children, to bring up and educate another generation. They'll bend to life's pressures, they'll give to each other's need—and they'll grow.

Ready or not

It is normal to grow. We begin life as helpless infants, completely dependent upon other human beings for our survival, and it's a long way from there to an independent, self-sufficient existence. Some people never make it. They get slowed down or stopped along the way, and part of them may linger behind.

Traditionally, most people have a Pollyanna attitude toward human development. In our culture we look only at the biological side of our beings, assuming that we all grow into adulthood by a certain chronological age. By that time each of us is expected to have passed through a variety of phases during which he has learned to handle the situations and master the skills appropriate to each age. A child of three, for instance, is expected to be able to walk, talk, and be weaned from the bottle. He's expected to be independent of his mother in some ways, but still dependent in others. The five-year-old supposedly is ready to separate from his mother and spend a few hours each day in kindergarten, where he learns to get along with other children. And so it goes, a pattern for each step along the way to an arbitrary chronological age, such as eighteen or twenty-one, by which time a human being is considered developed and able to make a life for himself.

So much for man's traditional view of human development. What really happens is another story.

Maturity is a process that is biological, emotional, and mental. It begins with birth and, with luck, continues until we die. There never should be a time when we've learned all there is to know. Maturation is an ongoing process, and as such, no one is fully mature. Maturity is a relative term, never a completed state.

Growth is more than learning. It involves change as we respond to our environment and to the other human beings in it. Gradually, through our reactions to our world, we become aware of how we respond to other people and to the situations of our lives. We learn what we can handle and where our limitations are.

A relatively mature person knows himself. He doesn't kid himself into thinking he's somebody else, no matter how appealing another personality may be. He accepts what he is. From having communicated with himself, he knows what he needs, and how he's likely to behave. He is aware of his feelings and he expresses them openly, without guilt. While he may not like the way he behaves in some situations, he can tell when he's made a goof, and when he finds out why he did it, he's able to change. But he doesn't worry about what he'll do the next time —he knows he's human and fallible, not divine. He lives spontaneously.

Such a person is for the most part at home with himself. He neither condemns nor glorifies what he is. He respects himself, and because he does, he respects what others are. In his openness, he can relate to other human beings, and he reaches a point where he wants to share his life with one of them.

Everything that he has experienced before in his life will enter marriage with him. Every feeling, situation, and person that has touched his life is part of him. It's the same with his spouse. Their different pasts will be very much a part of their future. And while in some cases they may know themselves, they can't possibly know each other fully. This they will have to discover within the framework of the marriage itself.

Why some people don't mature

Not everyone matures. While their bodies may be fully grown, some adults are like teen-agers, trying to act older than they feel. But unlike the teen-ager, who, under most circumstances, will outgrow his childlike ways, the immature adult's growth has been arrested.

We mature one step at a time. By discovering what he can do and by satisfying his needs at the age of three, a child is ready to move on to other challenges at age four.

Each stage of our development leads to the next, and each one depends upon the successful completion of those that came before it. We can't skip any stages and expect to get away with it.

It is a mistake to assume that all people finish one stage of growth before going on to another. It is also a mistake to expect all adults to be mature. Some people—many people—skip some stages in their development. Some go only part of the way toward maturity and no further, and they may spend the rest of their lives trying to cover it up. They may act out roles that are alien to their real needs, and all the while there is a child inside them having one hell of a time handling the adult-sized situations they meet.

There are many things that can arrest or slow our emotional growth. A baby's biological makeup and its influence on his temperament has a lot to do with the way he tries to make his needs known—and this, in turn, influences the way people respond to him. Some babies are very demanding, some are passive. Some parents are proud of an outgoing, aggressive child, others consider him a pain in the neck. Some babies have an easy time getting through to their parents, others meet resistance.

When we talk about a baby's environment, we mean, in part, the kind of parents he has. Are they cold, ungiving people? Are they overly warm and generous to the point where they smother him? Do they overprotect him or overfeed him? Do they ignore him? Are they aware that he wants to grow? Are they sensitive to his signals that he's finished with one stage of development and ready to go on to the next? Or do they hold him back, like the mother who keeps her child on the nipple until he's three or four years old? Are they interested in what kind of a person he'll become, or are they trying to force him into an uncomfortable behavior pattern, like the parent who turns toilet training into a battle of wills?

The size of the family and where the baby fits into it can slow down his growth or speed it up. The oldest child, especially if he is a boy, may get more attention because his parents have more time for him. He may also be especially sensitive to their unfulfilled desires and feel that he has to live them out in his own life. The youngest child may have to fight for what he wants, while the ones in the middle may be unsure of who they are and what they need.

All of these early influences can create obstacles to a child's emotional development. After all, a baby doesn't know who he is; he relies on others to tell him by their reactions to him. Is he lovable or despicable? Is he welcome in the world or will he have to battle his way in? He doesn't have the perception to make allowances for adults' hang-ups. He has to take their word for what he is—and the word sticks. If people react unfavorably to him, he gets a distorted image of himself. If every time he takes a step forward he gets stepped on, he'll resist growing because it is too painful. Instead he'll imitate the behavior of others his age, but he'll never really feel that he can keep up with them.

An immature person isn't sure of who he is. There is nothing he can call his own: not his actions, his way of speaking, nor even his way of thinking. He is a patchwork of mannerisms picked up from an assortment of other people, all of whom he feels are far superior to him. His capabilities have never been tested, and therefore he doesn't have any idea how far he can go with them. In fact, the most important thing he has learned in life is that he should avoid situations that may expose his deficiencies.

Meanwhile his real and unfed hungers keep demanding attention. The person he really is fights to get free and survive. Inside the tensions build up, increasing his self-contempt.

An immature person can't accept what he is, not only because he hasn't developed into a recognizable personality, but because he sees himself as unlovable. What else do all those early rejections mean but that he was an unlovable child? He condemns what he is, and while he can't change himself, he tries to disguise himself. He hides his real feelings because he thinks they, too, must be wrong. When they occasionally elude his control and break into the open, he feels a terrible guilt for exposing them to view.

Such a person has no respect for himself. He is angry with himself for being what he is, and angrier still with anyone who might penetrate his façade. Unable to make friends with himself, he also cannot relate to others. He only pretends.

Some of these pretenses are familiar: the man who won't let his wife work because he wants to prove that he's a good provider and therefore an adult; the penny pincher and the big spender, both of them in their different ways trying to prove that they're grown up and successful; the girl who rushes into an early marriage and motherhood to prove she's a woman. These people are out of touch with their feelings. What they do usually has no connection with what is going on inside them. Instead, the trigger for their behavior is somewhere in their past. What they do today is a reaction to what they felt in some distant, forgotten yesterday.

The stopped clock

If a person's emotional growth was stopped at an early stage of his life, part of him may go on to maturity, but other parts don't, and so in certain areas of his life he will continue always to react in a childlike way. The five-year-old girl whose father constantly breaks promises will be unable to rely on people in authority as she grows up. In her marriage, during times of stress, she may suddenly begin to mistrust the husband who is undeniably faithful to her. The little boy whose mother fought against his independence by reciting "all the things I've done for you," will be unable to pull away from mama. To him, living his own life is the same as betraying the woman who gave him "everything." God help his poor wife, and the in-law problem she will inherit!

These are fairly simple examples. The following is a typical description of the stuck personality:

KEN

Inside, Ken felt like a baby crying for his mother, yet he tried to act like a man. But he *was* a baby, still crying for the love he never got from his mother, who, together with Ken's father were remote, disinterested parents who sent him away to boarding school at the age of six. Being separated from his home before he was ready for his independence, he felt isolated and abandoned. From then on, every facet of his life was dominated by his attempts to get the approval and security he had been denied at that young age. He was stuck.

To protect himself from discovery, Ken picked up a lot from the other boys at school. He imitated what they did and how they spoke. He did it so well that no one guessed how frightened he felt as he went on to a more and more demanding life. He went through all the required motions of being a man. He graduated from college, got a job, married, and raised a family, but he was in no way equipped to take on the responsibilities of adult life. The business world was a threat to him because he thought he could never compete successfully with other men; he was too eager for approval and too afraid of rejection to take the risks necessary to moving ahead in a career. Fortunately, his family left him some money, enabling him to live on the level of more aggressive men.

Ken married a wealthy woman, partly out of his need for security. His wife also was domineering and aggressive, and he came to her for help with every decision and problem. But if he thought she would mother him—and he did—he was disappointed. Because she needed love as much as he did, she was unable to give him any. Hurt by Ken's attempts to lean on her, she constantly reminded him that she was more competent than he was. She had contempt for his volunteer work, which only made him look busy. Why didn't he put more time into his job and make more money?

Rejected, unsatisfied, Ken turned to other women, still looking for the mother he never really had. Of course he never found her. His wife, aware of his infidelity, came down with one illness after another, using her poor health as another excuse to withhold love.

Fixation can be more subtle than it appears in Ken's life. Many men with the same empty feeling inside them manage to hold down responsible, competitive jobs, covering up their deficiencies with a compulsive need to work. But on the weekends, they may become alcoholics, gamblers, or compulsively promiscuous.

Returning to the scene

Some people are able to grow in spite of handicaps. No matter how great the demands, or how aggravating the frustrations in their early life, they seem to push ahead to maturity. But there may be defects in their growth. It's not that they're unable to function as adults; they just find it very difficult. Under pressure they may revert to being a child, because they're not confident of their ability to handle some situations as an adult. The wife who runs home to mother after arguing with her husband is regressing to her childhood behavior. So is the man who overeats when he's lonely. It's easier for these people to deal with what was familiar to them as children than to face a new situation.

BETTY

Betty was convinced that everyone was out for himself because that's the way everyone in her family behaved. Mama took, but never gave. Papa worked nights and slept days; his needs were simple and he spent his life indulging them. He was a stranger to his family.

There were other problems in Betty's life. Not

really knowing a father, she created one in her mind. He was like God, all-powerful and able to give her anything she needed—except, of course, the fulfillment of her sexual desires. Because he was God, and because he was also her father, she didn't dare to look to her fantasy figure as a sex partner. In fact, she tried to do without sexual desires, to the extent that the very thought of sex made her ill. Love was all right, but purely on a nonphysical level. She married because, as St. Paul said, it's better to marry than to burn, but her husband was a cold, unresponsive man. Nevertheless the man was still a man, and Betty experienced sex. She hated it because it revived so many guilt feelings associated with her strict upbringing. She wished her husband wouldn't come near her. His physical appetites made him repugnant to her—he was in no way the asexual, godlike figure of a man she had conceived in her childish mind. Finally, she developed vaginismus, a condition in which her vagina became so tight that intercourse was painful, almost impossible.

When Betty went to a gynecologist, he referred her to a psychotherapist. Not expecting much, she went to him a few times, but in her eyes the psychotherapist, like everyone else, was out for himself. He wasn't interested in her problems; he only wanted her money. Then he made the mistake of doing her a small favor, and suddenly Betty's world came falling down on her. Things weren't going the way they always had when she needed help in the past; now she was actually getting it! She was in a totally new kind of situation, and that, on top of all the other pressures in her life, was more than she could take.

She had never learned how to react to someone who gave. It meant that she too had to give, and she didn't know how. The easiest way out was to go back to behaving like a child meeting a new and demanding situation. She cried and ran out of the office.

Over and over

While the more mature person can learn from his mistakes, the less mature person keeps making the same ones over and over. He avoids situations that threaten him with demands on his abilities, yet he tends to relive the bitter, painful events that crippled him. This is not his attempt to learn how to handle something difficult; instead it is his compulsion to repeat the unpleasant past in order to prove to himself that what he felt the first time was true for all time. You can see this quite clearly in the number of divorced persons who marry people very much like their first partner. You can see it in the husband who periodically beats his wife, making it impossible for her to live with him; or the wife who keeps telling her husband to leave—until he does. Something that happens in the present recalls an incident in the past, and while others may not see any similarity in the events at all, the troubled person is compelled to make the unpleasant thing happen again. He pushes the situation closer and closer to the brink until, in spite of warnings, he goes over the edge. Actually, he feels safer that way.

He may be a mystery to others, but he makes very good sense to himself. Faced with a frightening situation whose outcome is uncertain, he attempts to gain control of it. If the axe is going to fall, he wants to pick the spot where it will land. The wife who baits her husband by bringing up subjects she knows he despises is a victim of compulsion. She *wants* to make him blow his top. The husband who keeps lying to his wife *wants* her to leave him. What these people are really saying goes something like this: "You're going to reject me sooner or later. One of these days I'll do something that makes you so mad you'll want to get rid of me. It's going to happen, I know it, and I just can't stand waiting for it. So before it happens outside my control, *I'll make it happen.* Then I'll be on top of the situation."

For instance:

SUE AND GEORGE

They were young and very unhappily married. They fought bitterly and frequently, usually for the same reasons. George played around with other women, and always close to home. The last time he had an affair, it was with a friend of Sue's who eventually told her about it. When Sue confronted George, he seemed almost relieved. He was extremely remorseful, begging Sue to forgive him, willing to agree to any terms she might set for his future behavior.

Sue was cruel. She wanted a blow-by-blow account of the affair, complete with all the details of the lovemaking. She stopped eating and lost weight, and when people told her that she didn't look well, she said George was making her miserable. Yet she stayed with him.

Sue knew George would do the same thing again, and so did he. Perhaps it would be the woman next door. Who knows? Anyway, he wouldn't go far. He seemed to want Sue to catch him in the act, as if he wanted to flaunt his infidelity in her face and say,

"There! It was going to happen anyway, so I made it happen!" George, of course, didn't see it that way. He claimed that he couldn't help what happened. In fact, he blamed it on Sue. He said she was cold and sexually unresponsive, while the other women in his life gave him the love and warmth he needed. Actually that wasn't true, at least not wholly. She *was* unresponsive, but so were the other women George chased. That was the type he liked because they enabled him to cause the very rejection he feared.

ANNE

Anne is a very demanding woman who constantly wants to be fed. As she sees it, she was deprived of love in her childhood because her mother favored her sister. Now she feels life owes her everything.

As a child Anne rebelled against her mother's preference for her sister. To her it meant that she was being told to give up her individuality and imitate her sister. Distasteful as she assumed her personality was, she fought to preserve it. She tried to be whatever her sister wasn't, rejecting whatever her sister was. Her sister's black was Anne's white; her yes was Anne's no. Instead of preserving her real self, however, rebellion has distorted Anne into a negative, contrary, disagreeable person.

To justify the chip she carries on her shoulder, Anne provokes injustices and invites rejection. She is impossible to satisfy. She has a responsible job as an assistant controller for a large company, but her staff has a fast turnover because she is unable to get along with her employees. Impatient with beginners, she undermines their self-confidence by picking on the slightest flaws in their work. People who perform well become thorns in her side because she feels threatened by their competency. If anyone approaches her in a friendly manner, she is suspicious.

Anne has had a lot of good breaks in her adult life, but she can't afford to acknowledge them, and still goes on hating her mother and sister. The war she carries on against them depends upon her remaining miserable.

I (?) Thee (?) wed

We all bring to our marriages all the experiences and influences of our previous life. But along with what we have been, we bring with us the image of what we *think* we are. Ken saw himself as a man, yet he behaved like a child; his wife saw herself as a helpless little girl, yet she was capable of pushing her husband around. Betty, who couldn't give, saw herself as being taken. Anne, who cried out for affection, spurned it. The question is, Will the confused person choose a marriage partner who is also inconsistent with his declared needs? Probably so.

Ken complained that his wife was domineering, yet he needed her aggressiveness to make up for the lack of it in his own life. A more passive woman might have required a more decisive man, and Ken certainly wasn't one. Ken's wife complained that he was too dependent on her, yet she needed a man she could control. A self-reliant man might have exposed her inability to give love.

Some of us seek mates who will help us carry out the role we feel compelled to play. Consequently it's not unusual for us to attract someone who is also playacting.

Then we have the marriage of two complete strangers, neither of whom knows his own or the other's real self.

Marriage presents couples with completely new and untried situations, calling for the greatest amount of flexibility to meet them. Each partner must be willing to change, to adapt, to draw on what he has learned from his previous experiences, and to accept the fact that he will make mistakes. Because life now revolves around two individuals, each must be willing to give to each other's need and to take from each other's offerings.

If both partners in a marriage are emotionally immature, they will be threatened rather than stimulated by the newness in their life. They have entered marriage in the same way they entered each stage of their lives: with fear, insecurity, and a preconceived image of what they are expected to do. Distrustful of their feelings, they will be unable to learn through them what is going on inside themselves or inside each other. Therefore, they will be unable to grow. Instead, they'll be locked into their rigid ideas of how a husband and a wife are supposed to behave, and when each partner fails to live up to the expectations of the other, their world will start coming apart. Suddenly the child in them will appear, terrified, angry at being exposed, totally unequipped to repair the damage—and confused by the other child he finds facing him across the debris.

We all love the story that ends with "and so they lived happily ever after." Yet it is the beginning of the story that determines the end. How two people come together to share a marriage decides what kind of a marriage they will have and whether it will last. As we shall see, the reasons why couples marry are often unknown to the partners themselves.

6

Why Marriages Break Down

To understand why some marriages succeed and others fail we have to understand what brings a man and a woman together. Marriages don't happen by accident; they are the result of interacting human needs.

Have you ever wondered what your neighbor sees in her husband, or your boss in his wife? Or why the sexpot married the cold potato? Maybe you can't understand what they see in each other, but it's there. Or at least it was there in the beginning.

Need meets need

A mature person marries when he's ready to take on the responsibilities of a shared life. Until that time, and until he becomes aware of what he needs in a mate, he may meet several potential marriage partners, yet nothing happens. That's because he's busy taking care of other basic needs in his life. He may want to finish his education, get started in a career, or perhaps he just wants to become completely independent of his parents before taking on the responsibilities of his own home and family. In short, he's developing as a person.

The desire for a shared, intimate life with someone of the opposite sex is natural. The question is, With whom do we seek to share this life? Will we be drawn toward the kind of mate who can satisfy our needs or toward one who will taunt and frustrate us?

Many individuals haven't progressed to that point in life where they can accept themselves, and they aren't capable of taking on new responsibilities. Yet they marry to gratify their infantile needs and to convince themselves that they are adults. In fact, the primary cause of marital breakdowns is the emotionally underaged couples who marry. Children who dress up in their parents' clothes may stumble around in the oversized shoes and trip over the long pants and skirts. Immature men and women trying to assume adult responsibilities have far more disastrous falls.

Getting to know you

Dating and courtship are clumsy preparations for marriage because they encourage men and women to present a distorted image of their real selves. All of us want to be loved and accepted, and so we may tend to play down whatever we think will detract from our desirability in the eyes of the man or woman we want to impress. A sloppy man may come on like Mr. Clean, a bitch-on-wheels may seem like a kitten. It takes time for us to penetrate one another's façades, to react to one another's personalities and behavior, and gradually to reveal our innermost needs.

Unfortunately, not everyone has the perception to see what exists beneath the façade. Many people cover their real needs with endless layers of denial and repression, making discovery almost impossible, especially by another immature person. They also allow their infantile needs to distort their perception of others. For instance, a girl who deeply needs financial security may convince herself that a wealthy young man has other desirable qualities that actually don't exist. She wants him to be Mr. Right, but when it turns out that he isn't, she may be quite indignant. The deception was hers, however, not his, and she's lucky if she finds out *before* getting married.

Getting what we want

In every marriage there are two contracts: one apparent, the other subtle, even hidden. In the apparent contract, the man and woman agree to share their life for reasons that are obvious to them and to others. These are their conscious needs, and in this contract they vow to gratify them in each other. The subtle contract is negotiated on the unconscious level, where a couple attempt to fulfill their innermost desires. While neither one may be aware of what those desires are, their lives will be shaped by them. The more integrated person is more accepting of himself as a total being. That's because his inner self has developed along with his physical self, and what you see is what he is. For example, the kind of a man who consciously wants an intimate relationship with a woman is usually a person who has relatively few unconscious hang-ups about being close to another human being. Unconsciously, in some of his dreams, he may participate in sexual experiences that leave him relaxed and happy. Consciously, he will gravitate toward a woman who is affectionate on both the conscious and unconscious levels. Since this couple's unconscious needs aren't going to conflict with what they know they want from each other, they can enjoy a satisfying relationship.

The less secure person has a different experience. Because his unconscious needs are so far apart from the conscious needs he pretends to have, he has a hard time trying to satisfy them both. Unconsciously, such a person may dream of sexual activities that are interrupted by something threatening or frightening. On the conscious level, however, he may convince himself that he has a strong desire for intimacy with a woman. But because something earlier in his life arrested his emotional growth, the child inside him fears the closeness of another person. The woman this man seeks will have to be one who'll settle for a strange bargain, because his proposition goes something like this: "Let me *say* that I want to get close to you, but don't let me do it, because I *really don't* want to. Keep away from me, but let me complain that you're cold." In order to meet his conflicting needs the woman who would marry him would probably also fear warmth and intimacy, while at the same time telling herself that she wanted a man. She'd be the kind of wife who complained about her husband's impotency, when all the while she really wanted him that way.

Room for error

A person's perception is more accurate the more closely he is in touch with his own feelings. He won't fall for the put-on. He may put his best foot forward while trying to impress someone, but his other foot won't be far behind. He's a "together" person, and he'll want satisfaction on both the conscious and unconscious levels of his being.

For others, however, the tension between real and imagined needs is so strong that it keeps these people locked in that precarious position. Such an individual is not only blind to his own needs and abilities, he is unable to perceive them accurately in another person. In the expectation that someone can help him play the part of an adult on the conscious level of his life, he may fool himself into thinking that the same person also will be able to take care of the child secluded in his unconscious mind. He probably will be wrong. Assuming that he can satisfy what his chosen partner *says* she wants from him, he may not realize that he is deaf to what she really needs. The stronger his inner needs and the more they conflict with his surface needs, the greater the distortion in his perception. That's why, after marriage, spouses often seem to change. Actually they perceive each other differently. For instance, the man who marries a soft, dependent woman may be shocked to discover that she also has a sharp tongue when provoked. The woman who was attracted by a man's good manners and apparent considerateness may feel cheated when she perceives, after marriage, that he also is stingy. Depending upon whether these posthoneymoon discoveries feed or frustrate a couple's inner needs, the marriage will be strengthened or weakened.

What's that you said?

We can't go by what people *say* they want in a husband or wife. What they mean may be totally different. One woman who says she wants a strong man for a husband may really mean it; her conscious and unconscious needs may be identical. Another may be saying, "I want a strong man I can compete with and emasculate," expressing a conflict between her conscious and unconscious needs. The first woman may come from a family where the father was the strong partner, a man her mother depended upon for protection and security. She herself may feel comfortable in a dependent role, and therefore she won't be blinded by a man who puts on a show of maturity to cover up his basic inadequacies. A man will have to offer *real* satisfaction to both her inner and surface needs, for they are very similar.

The other woman is in trouble. She may come from a family where the father was a passive partner and the mother was a hostile, emasculating wife. The woman says she doesn't want a marriage like her parents', but she's heading straight for it. Fearing that she won't be acceptable as a castrating female, she can't come right out and admit what she wants. She can't even face her needs because her envy and hatred of men expose her discomfort as a woman. So she covers up by saying, "Sure, I want a strong man," but what she's really looking for is the man the other woman would have rejected —the put-on, the man who comes on strong to cover his weakness. Together they can pay lip service to his strength and her dependency; together they will feed off each other's repressed needs: hers to castrate, his to be controlled and manipulated.

Because it is not possible to satisfy conscious and unconscious needs at the same time, and through the same marriage partner, many a man faces a sad choice: satisfy one and frustrate the other. Actually, it isn't a choice at all, because what he does will depend upon the pressures exerted by his inner desires at the time he marries. If they are demanding attention, he will choose a mate to satisfy them, even if it means that he has to contradict his pretended desires. If his inner needs are sufficiently repressed, he will ignore them and seek a mate who complements the role he is playing—ignoring the very real possibility that his basic needs may, at some later time in his life, demand satisfaction.

The discrepancy between what people say they want and what they really need can therefore account for your neighbor's husband, your boss's wife, and many other marital combinations that seem incongruous on the surface. Actually the congruity runs very deep. A man who says, "I want a beautiful wife," may mean "I want a woman who will fit in with the good things I feel about myself as a human being." But another man may mean, "I want a Venus who can cover up my feelings of inferiority." One woman who marries a successful man may really want security along with the other qualities the man offers. But another woman may want a successful man only because she needs someone who can afford to pamper her and gratify her infantile desire for a father.

Sleeping in the beds we've made

From what we've been saying you might get the impression that everything works out all right in the end. With need seeking need, we may find some strange combinations among couples, but everyone gets what he or she wants—right? Wrong. They may be satisfying only their conscious *or* their unconscious needs, and that is not enough to sustain a marriage.

This doesn't mean that a man and a woman have to be perfectly suited to each other in every way in order to have a good marriage. But the more they can fulfill each other's core needs, and the more they are aware of those needs, the greater their chances for harmony. For example:

HELEN AND PETE

The unconscious needs of this man and woman are very similar to their conscious needs. Helen is perfectly comfortable being dependent upon her husband, and Pete enjoys giving her the support and strength she needs. Neither asks more than the other can give. Pete makes the major decisions in their life, but Helen's preferences are always respected. This couple has a good, active sex life, both of them enjoying their mutual ability to arouse and fulfill their desires. In short, these two people can accept themselves and each other for exactly what they are. The give-and-take they experience has also enabled them to grow.

Sometimes, when they can't satisfy each other's needs directly, they do it vicariously. It happens quite unconsciously. For instance, recently they had their house painted and the painter did a very poor job. Helen is meticulous about the way their home looks, and naturally she was upset. She didn't feel comfortable about complaining to the painter, although she was quite capable of doing it if she had had to. She thought Pete could deal with the painter more effectively than she could, and Pete quite agreed. He called the painter and insisted that the work be redone, which pleased Helen very much.

In this case Pete wasn't able to satisfy his wife's desires for a lovely home directly, which would have meant painting the house himself. Instead he did it vicariously through the painter. When Helen allowed him to complete his response to her needs by insisting the painter do a better job, he too was satisfied. You might say that everyone, with the exception of the house painter, was happy with the way this situation was handled.

Of course Helen and Pete are a rare couple in that their conscious and unconscious needs don't conflict. The "odd" couple is much more common in many marriages, but if a couple's conscious and unconscious needs aren't too far apart, they can make each other quite happy. For example:

MARGE AND HARRY

Marge likes pretty things and unconsciously wishes she had more money to spend on them. But consciously she's a practical, sensible, frugal woman who sticks to the budget. Harry, her husband, is the extravagant one. Now and then he puts them in the red by buying an expensive gift for Marge, who feels both guilty and pleased about accepting it. She's pleased about the gift itself, which satisfies her unconscious appetite for pretty things, and a little guilty about going over the budget. But the discomfort is small and the pleasure is great because Harry doesn't do these things on a large scale. If he were a compulsive big spender, they'd have a problem, not only because he would be trying to live up to a false image of himself, but because his constant gratification of Marge's desire for more money would eventually conflict seriously with her conscious need to be practical. Fortunately that isn't their situation. They can live with their discrepancies.

ELLEN AND RICHARD

Richard, even more than George Washington, can't tell a lie. But his wife can and occasionally does, especially when it comes to getting them out of social engagements they don't want to keep. Richard is a busy lawyer, fiercely honest and ethical. He works very hard, and at the end of the day he just wants to come home and put his feet up. Sometimes he doesn't feel like going to a party that he and Ellen planned to attend, but he isn't capable of inventing an excuse to stay home. That's when Ellen gets on the phone and does her thing. She tells a little white lie to get them out of the date, and Richard never criticizes her for it. In fact, they both know that secretly he is pleased with Ellen. That's because she is giving vicarious satisfaction to his unconscious desire to unbend, yet she isn't disturbing his conscious desire to be a truthful person. Ellen's guilt about telling a lie is also minimized by Richard's appreciation for her help.

If Ellen were a compulsive liar, and if Richard's desire to be truthful were simply a cover-up for his inner longing to be deceitful, their conflicting needs would create an unbearable tension in each other.

However, the discrepancies between their conscious and unconscious needs aren't great enough to keep them from interacting comfortably.

Sometimes a mate can frustrate his partner's unconscious needs and make them both happy. For instance:

PAT AND ARTHUR

Pat is on a diet that she finds hard to live with because unconsciously she doesn't want to lose weight—she'd rather indulge herself by eating. Consciously she wants to look attractive, but it isn't easy for her and she needs Arthur's help. One evening, for instance, she had a yen for a chocolate malted. After struggling with her compulsion for hours, she gave in and asked Arthur if he'd mind going out to get her a malted. Arthur smiled, but refused. He kissed Pat on the nose and reminded her that she was on a diet. He also told her that she was getting thinner and prettier every day, which encouraged her to exert her willpower.

Pat wasn't angry with her husband. Actually, her request for a malted was a test to see whether Arthur was holding to his part of their unspoken marriage contract. In other words, one of Pat's greatest needs was for Arthur to frustrate her more destructive appetites. He in turn was perfectly willing to satisfy that need. While their friends may think that he's a little too strict and she's a bit careless about herself, these two people *are* meeting each other's basic needs, causing only minor frustrations.

It's the marriage that attempts to meet the conflicting needs of the partners that becomes uncomfortable, especially when a hidden need doesn't show up until the honeymoon is over. For example:

CAROLYN AND JIM

Jim wanted an intelligent, well-educated wife to complement his image of himself as a successful businessman. That's what he got in Carolyn. The trouble is, Carolyn is too restless to be happy with housework and motherhood, especially now that their two children are in high school. She wants to resume the career she gave up when she and Jim were married, but Jim doesn't agree. He's really quite upset about her wish to return to work. Unconsciously, Jim isn't very sure of himself. He suddenly feels threatened by the emergence of abilities in Carolyn that seem to compete with his. Confused by his own unreasonableness, he refuses to permit his wife to work, using the excuse that people will think he isn't a decent provider.

In this marriage there is no room for working out the problem because Jim has frustrated a basic need in Carolyn. She doesn't want to compete with him; she simply wants to make better use of the abilities he found so attractive in her when they met, and she is deeply hurt by his opposition. This marriage is in trouble because the needs of the partners are shifting, some of them becoming more important than others. The marriage won't necessarily come apart, but an important need has been left unfed. As time goes on, the discrepancy between what Jim is and what he appears to be may cause Carolyn even more frustration, and that, if it isn't relieved, could disrupt their marriage.

A bed of nails

With the possible exception of Jim and Carolyn, the other couples we described were ready for marriage. The discrepancies between what they said they wanted and what they meant were minor and far from capable of destroying their enjoyment of each other. The partners are flexible people. They continue to grow, even if they have to grow around some small needs that aren't being met. They are well enough acquainted with themselves and with each other to sense when they are making a mistake, and they have enough self-respect to seek the reason for it.

When there is a serious gap between what people say they want in a marriage and what they really need, the couple lie stretched out on a bed of nails where each wrong move becomes excruciating. If their whole relationship is based upon their need to deny, repress, and frustrate each other, their complaints about each other often reveal clues to the conflicts within themselves. For example:

> Complaint: All my husband wants is sex. He's always after me, trying to make me do the most perverse things.
>
> Translation: I know I'm not really desirable, so I'll do anything with him, as long as he makes me feel wanted.
>
> Complaint: My wife is no good in bed. She's frigid.

Translation:	What I really need is a mother, but you can't go to bed with your mother.
Complaint:	My husband is impotent. I think he's a homosexual.
Translation:	No man's going to push me around. Who do men think they are, anyway!
Complaint:	I can't trust my wife. She drinks too much and goes for anything in pants.
Translation:	I wish I could be less inhibited. I wish I could screw around.

The truth is, for all their complaints, the partners in these marriages have the kind of relationships they want. They are asking each other to frustrate or to satisfy vicariously the powerful inner needs that they dare not face. While these arrangements may work for long periods of time, the slightest variation in the partners' needs or in the uncontrollable situations in their life can threaten their marriage.

Real life

If marriage were a static way of life, perhaps a couple could lie on a bed of nails indefinitely. But even if a man or woman dare not change, life itself changes. The bed may roll, and if the persons in it can't roll with it, they're going to get hurt. Try as they may to avoid them, new situations will come their way. Some couples can deal with them. In fact, their mutual gratification becomes more complete, more pleasurable, with their increased growth and adaptability. As they get to know themselves and each other better, their sense of satisfaction is greater.

Other couples run from life in order to deny what they are. Growth threatens them with exposure, and as they are forced into new situations, they have a hard time maintaining their façade. Sometimes, in fact, a change is unavoidable, and that may violate their original marriage contract.

In a more mature marriage the birth of children and the raising of a family may be part of a couple's conscious and unconscious vows. But in a conflicted marriage the coming of a child represents a major change in the marital relationship, and this, in turn, may represent a threat to one or both partners. For instance, childbirth may be abhorrent to a woman who got married to feed her narcissistic desires. In spite of her conscious willingness to go through the pregnancy and delivery, she may unconsciously resent the baby's demands on her time and energy, the stretching of her body and, in the case of a Caesarean delivery, the scars that she thinks make her unattractive in her husband's eyes. She may even feel that her husband, by impregnating her, broke his unconscious vow to make her feel desirable. Similarly, some men who unconsciously want their wives to mother them may feel betrayed by the birth of a child who demands so much of the wife's attention and affection.

Illness is another unexpected situation that can affect the terms of a marriage. For example:

HARRIET AND PAUL

Every night, for as long as they were married, Paul had made love to Harriet. If she was tired, if she wasn't feeling well, if she had her period, or even if Paul seemed tired, it didn't matter. They made love. Harriet never complained about Paul's demands on her, although she rarely experienced a climax or any deep sense of pleasure. Unconsciously she believed that she was sexually unattractive, and she was grateful for Paul's sexual appetites because they seemed to prove that he found her desirable.

Before their marriage Harriet had slept around a lot, trying to prove to herself that she was attractive. She *wanted* a husband who made demands on her, and that's what she got. It didn't matter that Paul often abused her by reminding her that she had been "a whore." When they went to bed, he reached out for her. He couldn't seem to resist her.

Then Harriet came down with a vaginal infection, which meant that sex was out for a while. To Paul, this was a violation of their marriage agreement, because what he really wanted was quite different from what Harriet assumed she was giving him. Paul had deep homosexual yearnings, and he was using Harriet to cover them up. She didn't arouse him sexually; he could resist her anytime he chose, but he chose not to, because he needed constant, repetitive proof that he was a man.

When Harriet's physical condition prohibited lovemaking, Paul felt betrayed, exposed. He even accused Harriet of having an affair with her gynecologist. There was nothing Harriet could do or say to reassure him, because his hidden needs were so inconsistent with the apparent ones he presented to her before their marriage. Finally, the bed of nails became too painful for either of them to endure, and the marriage broke up.

In a mature marriage where the conscious and unconscious needs are similar, the husband and wife can adapt to the changes that illness forces upon their relationship. There will be new needs for each of them to discover and fulfill, but they will be able to bend to their new circumstances because they can accept the realities of their life.

Mobility is another pressure upon many marriages today. Men "on the way up" are often on the move. The strain is even greater on their wives, who have to pack up the children and the furniture and move with their husbands, leaving friends, family, and possibly a career far behind. This requires an adjustment to new locations, new people, new life-styles, which can be disturbing to all but the most stable personalities. If a wife needs roots for her stability, she's in trouble, because her husband may no longer be able to give them to her at the same time he is attempting to satisfy her needs for financial security.

Frequently someone comes up with the claim that money is the cause of most marital problems. This, at least, is what many divorced persons give as a reason for marital failure. What these people are really saying is that money is the reason why some people get married —and when they don't get what they expected, they want out.

Money means many different things to different people—power, security, strength, sexuality. To some, money may seem to be the thing that can make their fantasies come true. The self-indulgent woman who marries because she expects a husband to give her a beautiful house, impressive cars, and a high level of living will feel betrayed if her husband can't afford more than a three-room apartment. She may contribute toward saving for a house, but she'll resent having to do it. In her eyes, her husband is a failure who can't make ends meet without her help. Money, to her, represents love, and as far as she's concerned, her husband isn't living up to his promise to love her.

Some immature men who are compulsively tightfisted marry women who do their spending for them. These men get a vicarious thrill from their wives' "promiscuity," and while they may complain about the bills, they continue to pay them. They like being the stern father to the naughty little girl. A severe financial setback, however, could make it impossible for these couples to satisfy each other's needs. Very likely these marriages wouldn't survive such a crisis.

The breaking point

Marriages don't break up only because a need is unsatisfied or a vow is broken. The terms of the unconscious marriage contract are strict and call for each partner to live up to them, but they aren't unalterable. Some marriages hold up under the most grueling conditions. Women may refuse to leave husbands who tie them up, beat them, and heap abuse on them. Men may stay married to wives who openly sleep with every other man but them.

Depending upon a couple's flexibility, and depending upon the distance between their real and imagined needs, spouses can tolerate some disappointment in their expectations. If they are flexible, they can adapt to new circumstances in their life and changing needs in their mate. If they are rigid, they will find it more difficult, perhaps impossible.

What really determines the breaking point in a marriage is not the specific needs that are no longer being met, or even a couple's disappointment in finding that they were wrong to assume their needs would be met at all. The breaking point is determined by each partner's tolerance for frustration. This tolerance, in turn, is determined by each person's biological, social, and emotional history, his unique character traits, and the experiences of his past life. For instance, a detached, withdrawn individual will not react as intensely as a more sensitive person to a violated marriage contract. Naturally a person with greater flexibility and the capacity to grow will be much better able to handle frustration than a child masquerading as an adult.

Ending it

If faltering marriages could end abruptly, we might say, "Too bad, but it's just as well. Good riddance," etc. But often they don't. Most bad marriages take a long time to break down, and for the very reason they began: a great many people have a hard time facing reality. Even when their marriages turn out to be poor bargains, it isn't easy for them to accept the truth. In their poverty of self-respect they don't realize that there is an alternative to their misery. Instead, they attempt to keep up the façade, covering up not only their real needs, but the real condition of their marriage. As the discrepancy grows between the way life is and the way they want life to be, the tension between these two points gets tighter and tighter. Yet in the midst of these jangling vibrations, confused couples still try to "make marriage work." They simply aren't equipped to do it, but it's a long time before they find out. In the meantime they do more damage to their marriage, and to themselves and to each other.

Granted, there's a lot at stake in a marriage, and its failure can be difficult. If a person feels that a broken marriage will cost him his self-respect, or that it means there is "something wrong with him," he'll try hard to keep the relationship going. If a person feels guilt—justified or unjustified—for his own failure to satisfy a partner, he'll try to avoid a breakup.

Unfortunately, many marriages are turning into hate matches because the partners want to bypass these unpleasant consequences of admitting failure. Thus we have wives who bitterly reject their husbands, only to run after them when they finally walk out. We have husbands who brutally abuse their wives only to beg their forgiveness. And we have children growing up in homes where they see the worst examples of married life.

When some of these marriages do break down, the partners usually take the loss as a personal one. While each may blame the other for ruining the relationship, each partner is actually projecting his or her own sense of guilt and frustration onto the other. A more mature couple would be able to recognize much earlier that their marriage simply wasn't working out and that it would be best for both of them to end it.

Until recently our divorce laws reflected these personal feelings of bitterness, loss, guilt, and blame. One partner had to be labeled the victim, while the other was the one who did the hurting. Alimony payments and custody of children were more often settled along punitive lines than in the interests of the human beings involved.

Hopefully, the increasing acceptance of "no-fault" divorce laws means that society is ready to accept the fact that a man and a woman deserve compassion rather than blame when they find that they cannot live together any longer. As divorce itself is handled more rationally perhaps troubled couples will find it less painful to end a marriage that is working against them.

PART III

WHO'S CAUGHT IN THE MARRIAGE GAP AND WHY?

7

Couples Caught in the Marriage Gap

One evening, as two former college roommates were having a reunion in a favorite restaurant, one of the young women began to cry. She told her friend that she was so unhappy with her husband that she was thinking of suicide. She had been married for two years, and since the birth of her first child a year ago, her husband hadn't slept with her. He claimed that he didn't want to get her pregnant again because they couldn't afford more than one child at that time.

"Aren't you on the Pill?" her friend asked.

"No. We're both Catholic, so that's out."

"But there are other ways," the friend said.

"He's afraid to take the risk."

"Well, what are you going to do? If you're thinking of suicide, things must be pretty bad. I mean, what about a divorce?"

"Can't. It's the religion thing again."

The friend was at a loss to suggest anything that would help the young woman. When she left town that night to return to her home, she was deeply worried, fearing that her friend might do some harm to herself.

What the friend didn't realize was that her former roommate's marriage was fulfilling her unconscious needs, despite her apparent unhappiness. She was a very troubled girl who was afraid of sex, and she married a young man who had similar anxieties. Neither one was able to face his or her inner fears, so they unconsciously agreed to avoid sex. During the first year of their marriage it was the young wife who frequently rejected her husband's sexual advances, but the birth of a child presented a more convenient way out. Religion and the possibility of an unwanted pregnancy, however, were only the conscious excuses this couple used to cover up the fact that she was afraid a man would abuse her and he was afraid he was impotent. While they appear to be miserable with each other, they will probably stay married as long as their needs remain the same—which can be a very long time.

What we can see from the outside of a marriage may be very different from what is really happening. We often see only the façade a couple erects to hide their unconscious relationship from themselves. We see the conscious contract they made when they got married, and we are aware of the vows that have been broken as time goes on. We hear their complaints, their unhappiness and disappointment are obvious, but what we may not see are the real reasons these couples married and why they continue to live together. Infantile as their needs may be, as long as they satisfy them in each other, their marriage will work. The danger, of course, lies in the probability that one or both partners may change or outgrow their need for the other.

Couples Caught in the Marriage Gap

The following sketches of different marital contracts are taken from a psychotherapist's casebook. The identities of the couples have been changed to insure privacy and to protect the confidential nature of the consultation between therapist and patient. In these examples you'll be able to see the gap that has formed between the couples' unrealistic expectations and their unconscious needs. Trying to satisfy these inner needs without acknowledging them is often a complicated exercise in frustration.

"I NEED SOMEONE TO LEAN ON"

According to this wife, her husband never gives her anything she wants. Nor does he give her the strength she needs from a man. Every time she says, "I want," he says, "No." But her husband claims she wants too much. They both say they're completely dissatisfied with their marriage and would get a divorce if only they could afford it.

Unconsciously, however, he and she are living up to their agreement to relive their childhood experiences in which they were denied maternal love. So they will put up with any abuses in order to confirm their conviction that they are unlovable. They don't know how to give or take warmth and affection. Instead, the wife plays the part of the child, running to her husband with endless demands and pleas, and he plays the sadistic, denying mother, doing to his wife what was done to him. Each of them also gets a vicarious satisfaction out of the role the other plays.

"I need someone to hurt (me)"

"If it weren't for the children," this couple would have separated long ago, they say. Yet they've been at each other's throats for years, and the constant fury in their home has crippled their two children with severe emotional illnesses.

This husband and wife have an unconscious agreement to hurt each other, and if they were to stop, their marriage would probably end. He resents women and she hates men, and they need excuses to express these hostilities. Unfortunately the children are paying the price for their strange union. The eight-year-old is in an institution for emotionally disturbed children and the ten-year-old is in the custody of the Juvenile Court.

"I'll show you who's boss!"

He interprets everything as an attempt to manipulate him. If his wife suggests that the cellar needs cleaning, he thinks she is commanding him to do it. He's especially touchy if she mentions that something needs to be repaired. It bothers him that he isn't handy, because that's the way he thinks men are supposed to be, and he doesn't like to be reminded of his deficiencies. Worse still is when his wife fixes something. She's very good with tools, and he resents this and sees it as a direct attack upon his manhood.

Even when he has the time, however, he never does a thing around the house, but when his wife has to call in a plumber or an electrician, he gets furious. If she doesn't call for help and the pipes start leaking, he blames her for not taking care of the house. Either way, he makes a lot of noise.

His wife takes his tantrums quite calmly. Sometimes she even has a little smile on her face.

Although this husband protests that he doesn't want anyone to boss him around, in reality this is what he is trying to arrange. As a child he was overprotected by anxious, perfectionistic parents and never had a chance to put his abilities to the test. He feels inept, clumsy, fearful of making a mistake, more like a boy than a man, and the demands of adult life are more than he can handle by himself. He needs help from someone stronger, namely, his wife. By doing nothing, he forces his wife to do something. She submits her strength to him, and he overpowers her with his weakness. This, of course, is what his wife needs, too. She thinks men are fools, and she wants to compete with her husband to show him that she's the stronger of the two. She enjoys letting him blow off steam because she knows it's a sign of his weakness. That's why she smiles. She knows she's wearing the pants in this family, and so does he. But that's the way they want it.

"IT'S ALL MY FAULT, I KNOW IT"

Their life is dull, empty. They work at boring jobs, and when they come home they eat and watch TV until they fall asleep in their chairs. She blames him for it. She says he never tries to please her, never takes her out, never even sleeps with her anymore. He's inert and passive. When she throws this up in his face, he just nods and accepts the blame, which drives her up the wall. She knows he has no intention of changing.

But neither has she. This couple have a marriage that only *seems* incompatible. Before marriage both of them were withdrawn, isolated individuals, and they want to stay that way. In spite of the fact that they told themselves they were marrying a partner who would give them the love and warmth they had missed as children, an expression of real affection would be threatening to both of them. To accept it, they would have to come out from behind the wall they have built around themselves to avoid being hurt. That would be too risky.

And so they live their separate lives—together. He's happier not sleeping with his wife because he really wants to be mothered, and sex would only conflict with this desire. In his passive way he takes out his inner hostility on his wife by doing nothing more than earning a living. He also disarms her by accepting the blame for it almost before she can lay it on him.

She is responsible for some of their difficulties, too, although she can't admit it. She's afraid of sex, and the fact that her husband doesn't sleep with her anymore is fine with her. She can also satisfy her need for self-blame vicariously by blaming him for the emptiness in their life.

"IT'S ALL YOUR FAULT!"

Before he can open his mouth, she accuses him of picking on her. If he fails to read her mind, she calls him insensitive. If he doesn't want to make love when she does, he's impotent. If he wants to make love, she accuses him of humoring her.

He can't take criticism. When his wife complains that he spends his weekends fixing his car, he counterattacks by telling her she ought to give up her job and take care of their house. This kind of sniping can go on for days.

Both husband and wife are satisfying their need to put the blame for their problem on something or someone outside themselves. He was an only child brought up by doting, overcautious parents who never gave him a chance to develop and grow. He was afraid to do something wrong, because his mistakes were severely criticized. His wife had a similar childhood experience. She was the only daughter, and her four brothers were always teasing her and picking on her. Her parents did nothing to stop them or to protect her, and she grew up feeling that everyone was out to get her.

Unconsciously, both he and she believe that they deserve all the blame that was heaped on them, and their unconscious marriage contract calls for them to criticize each other severely. Their need is so strong that they see blame where there isn't any, and if one partner doesn't provide it quickly, the other will provoke it.

"I HAVE TO DO ALL THE GIVING"

She sees herself as a martyr, a slave to her self-indulgent husband. She has a night job so that during the day she can clean the house, cook the meals, do the laundry, and take the kids wherever they have to go. She even mows the lawn because she knows her husband won't do it. She never goes anywhere, and if she did she wouldn't have any decent clothes to wear. Her husband complains when she buys anything for herself, yet he spends a lot on his own clothes.

In bed she feels more like a concubine than a wife, for here again she has to do all the work. He simply lies back, waiting for her to stimulate him. Sometimes she'd like *him* to start a little love play, but he never does.

This woman brings her martyrdom upon herself. Her husband enjoys being pampered, but he'd probably do a few things to help his wife if she'd give him the chance. He might help with the dishes if she didn't rush to do them before he finished eating. He might mow the lawn if she didn't beat him to it at an ungodly hour in the morning. He might take her out if she ignored his objections and made herself more attractive. He might even agree to some domestic help, enabling her to get a daytime job, if she didn't insist that no one else could keep their house as well as she can.

The truth is, this woman chose to marry a self-indulgent man because he satisfies several conflicting needs in herself. She gets a vicarious pleasure out of his selfishness and at the same time she can be critical of the way he "gives in to himself." By waiting on him hand and foot, by doing without domestic help, by doing things before he has a chance to do them, she is satisfying her need to degrade herself. This, in fact, is the only kind of relationship she has ever known with a man. Even her husband's passive sexuality is gratifying to her because it makes her feel used.

Her husband's need to feel like a king is certainly gratified by such a wife. This man has serious doubts about his masculine capabilities and that's why he married this self-sacrificing, self-debasing woman. He needs to be reassured by her slavishness that he is attractive as a man, and she needs to feel that a man wants her.

"ANYTHING YOU CAN DO, I CAN DO BETTER!"

This couple is out to prove to each other that they haven't given up anything by getting married. He insists that it's his male prerogative to go out with his friends and come home late a few nights a week. She, as a liberated woman, demands equal time out. When he objects, she gets even by refusing to fix his meals. At parties she flirts with his friends, which infuriates him.

Their sex life is active, but not what you'd call satisfying. They seem to be more preoccupied with sexual positions than with sex itself, and they scrupulously keep track of who was on the top and who on the bottom last, so they can alternate. It's obvious that they are using sex as an opportunity to demean each other rather than to enjoy an erotic experience.

As a child he was dominated by his mother and rarely saw his father, who traveled a lot. His mother made it clear that she preferred his sister to him, and he grew up with hostile feelings toward women.

She was brought up by an overly submissive mother and a sadistic father who often beat her and humiliated her. Through her own experience and through the example of her mother she formed a very low opinion of women. She both envied and resented men.

While it seems that each partner in this marriage is trying to prove himself or herself superior to the other, their real relationship is quite different. Their need is not to surpass each other but to be proved an inferior person.

"MY MOTHER (MY FATHER) LOVED ME"

He works for his father, but only because his wife pushed him into the job. When they were married, he took a job that meant moving to another part of the country. His wife, who had never been separated from her parents, was miserable. She hated their house and the town they lived in, and refused to make any friends there. Finally he agreed to accept his father's offer of a job in the family business, and they moved back.

Now she sees her mother every day and calls her often. He's with his father all of his working hours. He complains that he never had a chance to prove himself, but she reminds him that he has a better job and more security than most men his age. They can afford a nice house and lovely furniture, although she complains that they don't live as well as she did with her parents. He responds by saying that the food was much better when he was with *his* parents.

Consciously, this couple appear to be dissatisfied with the bargain they've made. But unconsciously they are feeding each other's needs to be dependent upon their parents. According to their conscious marriage contract, he was expected to be a father to his wife, and she was to be a mother to him. By each of them failing to live up to these expectations, they fulfilled each other's need to continue to be a child.

"I'M (NOT) LIKE MY MOTHER!"

He says that his wife is withdrawn, almost disinterested in him. Yet at times—and for him, always the wrong times—she smothers him with affection, which he can't help but reject. Then she accuses *him* of being withdrawn.

Both these people grew up in homes where the father was aloof and the mother was hostile to the child. But instead of expressing their hostility openly, both mothers tried to cover it up by fussing over their children.

The husband's mother hid her feelings behind an elaborate concern for the boy's health, and in time he began to see himself as a fragile creature. In spite of his superior intelligence, his grades were poor. He made very few friends and rarely dated. His sexual experiences before marriage were negligible. In other words, he never pushed himself to get something he wanted.

His wife's mother took out her resentment of her daughter by overburdening her with family responsibilities and then finding fault with everything she did. The child had to do all the housework and look after her two younger sisters, whom her mother clearly preferred. Any resentment she felt was simply not tolerated, and every parental order was accompanied by the explanation, "Because we love you." The girl hated to be used as domestic help, yet her own resentment made her feel guilty. She didn't feel it was right to hate parents who kept telling her they loved her. But they certainly didn't show it. Her parents never hugged her or kissed her, and she hungered for the touch of affection. She thought she would get it from her husband.

In this marriage, the spouses are failing each other as far as their imagined needs are concerned. Nevertheless, they are giving each other the only satisfaction each can accept, and that is the chance to re-create the mother-child relationship they knew in their earlier years. The husband would be furious if anyone said he was just like his mother, but that's what he is in relation to his wife. He pulls away from her at the moment she lunges out at him with an affectionate grasp that is almost frightening. Then, when she withdraws, he blames her for ignoring him. Unconsciously he's telling her, "I know you really hate me, even though you say you love me. I know you want to choke the very life out of me. So I'll run from you to show you that you can't get to me. I'll use you, but I'll ignore you." His wife avoids any affectionate physical contact with her husband, which is exactly what her mother did with her. She doesn't want to get close to him because she's afraid of getting hurt again. She also senses the rage of resentment that lies just below the surface of her personality and fears that it might destroy him, and surely their relationship, if she ever relaxed her control over her feelings. Yet at times when she is overcome with loneliness and abandonment, she clutches at him in a frenzied attempt at love. It doesn't work. The more she clings, the more smothered he feels, and he pulls away from her—which is exactly what her mother did.

"BIG DADDY'S LITTLE GIRL"

He complains about the way his wife spends money. She goes on shopping sprees, throws too many parties, buys expensive food, and has to throw half of it away.

His wife says that he doesn't tell her the truth about their financial situation. She thinks he's stingy. One day he'll tell her they're broke, and that same night he'll bring home an expensive gift for her. If he can spend that kind of money, why can't she put decent food on their table?

His complaints are a cover-up for the pleasure he gets from his wife's spending habits. Her extravagance satisfies his unconscious need to be promiscuous without conflicting with his conscious need to control himself.

She was given too much as a child, and he was given too little. Now they're repeating those earlier experiences. By being the spoiled little girl, this wife indulges her husband's need to be extravagant and at the same time allows him to confirm his infantile opinion of women as takers, as ungiving creatures who withhold love and material things. The husband reciprocates by playing Big Daddy, the giver, the dispenser of gifts—but he's also the limiting, controlling, manipulator who keeps his little-girl wife from going too far.

"CALL ME CINDERELLA"

All her life this wife dreamed of making it big, of having lots of money, a beautiful house, and an exciting life. Her family had said she'd never amount to anything, but she'd show them! She'd get even for the poverty of those early years, for all the times she was slighted, for all the things she had to do without. Someday Prince Charming would come along and . . .

Now she complains that her husband is a failure and that marriage hasn't changed her life a bit. She's still poor, still doing without, still envying people with money while her husband does nothing about it.

This husband also comes from a poor family, and like his wife, he wasn't willing to follow the rainbow. Instead, he kept waiting for someone or something to dump the pot of gold in his lap.

These partners are unable to let their material needs motivate them into the kind of action that would improve life. Instead, they are fulfilling their unconscious need to blame each other for the barrenness of their lives.

"I NEED YOU, BUT WHO WANTS YOU"

She says she can't stand the way her husband gives in to her and does everything she wants. Doesn't he have a mind of his own? The other night, for instance, on their way home from the theater, she asked him to stop for a pizza, *and he did!* Yet he knows very well that she's trying to lose weight. He eats like a bird, but he lets her grow into a blimp.

He can't understand why his wife loses her temper with him, especially when he does something to please her. He says he likes to do things for her. It doesn't really bother him, either, that she's getting so fat. Let her enjoy herself.

This wife may have imagined that she wanted a stronger man for a husband, but she *needed* the one she got. She's a woman who has no control over herself. Her life is a compulsive effort to grab, take, eat, drink, manipulate. She says she wants someone to restrain her, but God help anyone who tries!

Her husband is a detached automaton of a man who gratifies his inner appetites through his wife. That's why he gives her anything she wants; it's his only way of indulging himself vicariously while playing the role of the self-denying man.

She reciprocates by making his decisions for him, which is something he isn't able to do for himself. Sometimes he senses that he's missed out on something, that maybe his life is too flat, but the feeling doesn't last long. He's not a particularly sensitive man, so he isn't disturbed by what he doesn't have.

He has his wife and she has him, which seems to be enough for both of them.

"What I Gave Up for You . . ."

To outsiders it seems that this couple got married just to snipe at each other. She never misses an opportunity to remind him of the successful men she *could* have married, the degree she *could* have earned if she hadn't dropped out of college in her senior year, and the fun she *could* have had as a single girl, all of which she gave up to marry him. He gripes about the world trip he never took, the graduate school he never attended, the career he would have preferred, and the girls—oh, the girls he could have had! But he married her instead.

Actually she didn't *want* to finish college, and he didn't *want* to go to graduate school. Unconsciously, they both were too insecure to carry out their plans. But this is something they can't admit to themselves, and so they blame each other for their failures.

"I Made You What You Are Today"

This husband thinks his wife ought to get down on her knees and kiss the ground he walks on, after all he's done for her. She was nothing before he married her. Her family was so poor she had to leave high school to work in a factory. Yet now she has the nerve to tell him *he* ought to get a job!

He doesn't have to work. His family left him so

much money that he can afford to spend his time looking after his investments, which he does. But his wife says he's lazy. She tries to keep him busy by asking him to mow the lawn and wash the car.

It would seem as if the wife is the one who elevated herself by means of marriage. In a subtle way, however, her husband is using her to make himself appear bigger, more powerful, and more successful than he really feels. He's a man who never had to test himself. Everything was given to him before he could even ask for it, so he doesn't know what he could do for himself if he had to. He's afraid it wouldn't be very much, and to defend himself against these inner doubts, he married a woman he considers inferior to him.

His wife married well, which is what she always wanted. She's the Cinderella gal getting back at the mean old sisters who said her feet were too big for the glass slipper. The only trouble is she feels guilty because she has so much while her family is still poor. When she visits her sisters, she can sense their envy, and she can't blame them. Why should she be the one to have so much? Especially when she agrees with her family that she's worthless. To punish herself, and to confirm her low opinion of herself, she wants her husband to get angry and remind her of her background. That's why she nags him about getting a job, and why she finds fault with everything he gives her. Her husband, by humiliating her, then feels that he has gained in stature. Need—however infantile it may be—is meeting need.

"LET ME COMPLAIN, AND DON'T TRY TO STOP ME"

She doesn't like the way he talks about her mother. He keeps promising to stop criticizing her, but if his wife just mentions her mother, he starts again.

He says his wife is just as bad when she complains about the size of their apartment and the way their neighborhood is deteriorating. He's sick and tired of hearing about their "ignorant" and "filthy" neighbors. He'd like a bigger apartment in a better part of town, too, but right now they can't afford it.

This couple is like George and Martha in *Who's Afraid of Virginia Woolf?* They constantly complain and then criticize each other for it. He *did* stop complaining about her mother, until his wife provoked him by bringing up the subject again. She *did* stop knocking their apartment, until he came home one night and mentioned how shabby the lobby looked.

In spite of their ostensible disagreements, these partners actually need each other's tirades. It's their way of letting each other express unconscious hostilities for them. For instance, the wife is suppressing her own resentment toward her mother because she's afraid of its destructive force. By provoking her husband into expressing anger for her, she doesn't have to feel guilty about it. She reciprocates by complaining about the way they live—which her husband also doesn't like, but can't admit because it reflects on his image of himself as a provider. When she says the neighborhood is deteriorating, he says it's not *that* bad, but he's saying it more to himself than to her. This husband and wife would be very frustrated if the outlet for their anger were to be closed off. That's why, when either partner stops complaining, the other one begins provoking.

"IF YOU'RE HAPPY, I'M SAD—IF YOU'RE DOWN, I'M UP"

This husband and wife are using each other to express their unconscious anxieties about themselves. She calls her husband a sourpuss. She says he hates to see her happy, and whenever she's enthusiastic about something, he's gloomy. Sometimes, when his pessimism drives her to tears, she swears she catches him smiling.

Unconsciously she welcomes her husband's restraining influence. Aware that her emotions are easily aroused, she is afraid they will get her into trouble, and she relies on her husband to keep her safe.

Her husband both fears and admires her emotional extravagances. Once it took him three months to pay the bills for one of her redecorating sprees, and recently she was so elated about their new dentist that she almost had an affair with him. Behavior like that causes him to react with panic when he sees that gleam in his wife's eyes. However, because he's afraid to experience a sense of release within himself, he lets her express it for both of them. When he's tense or in a depressed mood, he counts on his wife's joviality to snap him out of it. At times, though, he finds a sadistic satisfaction in reducing the amount of pleasure she feels. Yes, he does smile just a little when he can make her cry, but he doesn't even realize it—he's reacting to the relief he feels after expressing some of his pent-up hostility.

"How can you do this to me?"

This husband never complains about his wife, but his friends do. They call her a bitch and can't understand how he can live with her. She's always after him about something: either he doesn't make enough money, or he doesn't spend enough time with the children, or he's always saying and doing the wrong thing. If he protests, and he rarely does, his wife goes into a tantrum about all the abuse she's taken from him.

Beneath this husband's easygoing façade is a lot of resentment, not only against his wife but against his mother, who treated him the same way. His mother covered up her resentment of him by being overly protective. She gave herself away, however, in such morbid remarks as, "Wear your rubbers or you'll catch pneumonia and die," "Be careful with that knife or you'll cut your veins." She also was very critical of anything the boy did and expected more from him than he could achieve. Naturally, he felt like a failure most of the time. To avoid criticism he played the role of Mr. Nice Guy. To avoid failure he became a procrastinator. While he's a fairly successful accountant, he could do better if he didn't spend so much of his time shuffling the papers on his desk and going out for coffee. He also allows his clients to owe him money and he can't bring himself to insist on payment.

His wife wanted a husband she could emasculate in order to justify her contempt for men. She too expects more of her husband than he can possibly give her, which in turn enables her to call him a failure. She even tells him that his penis is too small.

Both these partners seek refuge in their individual fantasies where they have experiences that could never take place in their real lives. The husband often imagines his wife dead and himself in the arms of a gentle, loving, undemanding woman. The wife sees herself pinned down by a powerful man who releases her from the prison of her frigidity by raping her. How different their inner needs really are!

In reality this wife confirms her husband's unconscious feeling that he is weak and contemptible, which is the way his family treated him at a very early age. He offers his wife a man she can castrate and control, which in turn enables her to satisfy her need to feel superior to him. He is then able to satisfy his unconscious resentment of his mother by hating his wife.

"HAVE YOUR FUN, LITTLE BOY—YOU'LL ALWAYS COME HOME TO MAMA"

He's a charmer at parties. He's a fund of fascinating stories and information, and people who meet him admire him. His wife seems to be his only drawback. She's dull, straitlaced, and very unsociable.

Of course, she has her reasons to complain. Every now and then her husband has an affair, which he does little to conceal. But she always takes him back and forgets about it. "He has to have his little fling," she says, as if he were her son rather than her husband.

Actually, she gets more out of his "flings" than he does. Feeling as unattractive as she does, sex is uncomfortable for her, and she'd just as soon let another woman take care of her husband's sexual needs. Then, when he comes back to her full of guilt and remorse, he'll do whatever she wants.

This woman wanted a husband who needs mothering, and that's what she's got. She can't handle a grown man because she doesn't feel like a woman. She needs a boy.

Beneath all his charm, her husband is a child who plays at taking on a man's responsibilities. His only security comes from knowing that his wife will take care of everything, including him. Other women mean nothing to him because they can't (or won't) give him the mothering that he seeks. In fact, he has his affairs quite openly because they enable him to come home to his wife like the naughty little boy who wants to be forgiven.

"WHAT'S IN IT FOR YOU?"

In all the years they've been married, her husband never sent her a card for a birthday, an anniversary or any other holiday. Once he gave her a gift, but only once. She's been a good wife and mother, but her family doesn't seem to appreciate her. Not that she expects them to bow down and thank her for doing her job; she just wants a little recognition, that's all.

This husband admits that he forgets things like birthdays, but once when his wife reminded him about her birthday, he bought her a beautiful bracelet and got hell for it. She said he never would have done it if she hadn't shamed him into it.

This wife was a neglected child whose parents seemed to feel that she didn't deserve anything. Now, however, her life is quite different. Her husband and children have tried to express their appreciation for her, her friends have always been grateful for her helping hand, and she's been presented with more than one award for her charity work. These she chooses to forget because they make her uncomfortable. She really wants to convince herself that her parents were right about her worthlessness, and any attempt to give her something only proves that her parents were not only wrong, but cruel. This realization brings her repressed anger to the surface, threatening her with its destructive power. She must put it down.

In this woman's life there can be no give and take. She must be taken from, not given to—ever. That's why she married a passive man who is not especially sensitive to her hints about birthdays and words of praise. He in turn has an unconscious need to withhold himself from his wife, which is his quiet way of getting back at his own depriving parents.

Crying out for love and attention on the surface of their lives, this man and woman are really bound together by their agreement to give each other as little as possible.

"You never give me anything"

He says he gives his family everything, and they give him nothing. He sends flowers to his wife at her office, and she doesn't even say "thanks." He often slips the kids a few extra dollars, but when he needs their help around the house, they've got other things to do. He's a patsy, that's all.

When this man gives, he does it to get something back. If there's nothing he wants from his family, they don't get a thing from him. He thinks he does enough for them by earning a living. If he gives them more than that, such as flowers for his wife or money for his children, sure enough, he'll ask them for a favor. Usually he'll ask for something they can't give him, which means he'll be able to tell them how ungrateful they are.

His parents used to do the same thing to him when he was a child. They'd give him things, but only to make him feel obligated to them. Then, when they wanted something from him, he had to say yes. If he didn't—well, you can guess. Now, in his marriage, this husband is satisfying his need to be the blackmailing parent. His wife, who is a compulsive taker, obliges him by playing the ungrateful child.

In the long run

In these sketches we can see some of the most common ways in which many couples bridge the gap between their real and fantasized needs. Of course there are others, and endless varieties of them. We've also simplified the couples' frustrations, and looked at them one at a time. But in most marriages you'll find more than one.

Many of these marriages go on forever. In order for them to survive, however, neither partner can afford to change or grow or need anything more or less different than he or she is getting right now. Each has to suppress the human ability to adapt and mature. Each has to withstand the pressures of a society that is changing at a revolutionary pace. Each has to oppose change in his or her partner. Frankly, the prospects aren't good.

8

Marriages Bound by Fear

One of the urgent inner needs that drive confused people into marriage is a dark area that deserves some light. There are men who fear that they are not men, and women who fear that they are not women. Very often they marry to escape their fear, only to find that the fear itself has chosen their mate and is running their marriage.

While we speak more freely today about homosexuality *per se,* we're still tight-lipped about homosexuality in relation to everyday life. It's more comfortable for us to think of homosexuality as something on another planet, with an existence of its own. We can label it, analyze it, understand it, sympathize with it—all of which keeps us from considering the uneasy possibility that homosexuality may be interwoven into our own personal world. Does it perhaps exist in marriage? In *many* marriages? Are many married men and women actually latent homosexuals?

Many of them think they are.

As we have progressed beyond an agrarian society into a technological one, there are fewer lines distinguishing men from women, at least in the social sense. There are no longer such designations as "man's work" and "woman's work." A husband is not necessarily the breadwinner, nor the wife the breadmaker. Men and women often dress alike, do the same work, and share many of the same feelings. What a person does and where he or she does it no longer labels him or her a man or a woman. This sexual identity now must come from within the individual, and those who have inner doubts about it will get very little help from outward appearances.

Let's get one thing out in the open. If a person behaves in a homosexual manner, he's a homosexual. If he behaves in a heterosexual manner, he's a heterosexual. The same goes for bisexuality. It's not very likely, then, that you're going to find homosexuals living heterosexual married lives. What you do find is a lot of married people living in the *fear* that they may be—or may become—homosexuals.

Men who are unsure of their masculine capabilities have an especially rough time in this age of the liberated woman. It's not easy for them to play the part of the adult male when there seems to be no great demand for such things as muscles and physical strength, or when there are no longer such definitions as "man's work" and "woman's work." When a man is comfortable being a man on both a conscious and an unconscious level, he isn't going to mind helping his working wife keep their home presentable. A vacuum cleaner is no threat to his image of himself. But if he's the kind who has to prove his sexual identity by the things he does, he'll die before he'll move any dust out of his way. He sees the vacuum cleaner as his wife's accusation that he is more feminine than masculine, which is especially frightening because that's what he fears may be true. Since he doesn't really feel he's a man, he's always haunted by the possibility that he may be a woman.

Women also have their problems in our changing society. In spite of their increasing opportunities to develop as individuals, many hang back. Independence is a hard thing for a woman to handle unless she is secure and very much at ease with herself as a woman. If she is unsure of herself and feels that she must always behave in a passive, dependent way to be considered a woman, she'll resist any of her normal aggressive drives. They may make her look too "butch" in her own eyes.

While sex seems to be the problem here, it is really the symptom of an emotional handicap that cripples the whole person. Reconciling their real and imagined needs in a marriage will be difficult for these people, but they will certainly try. A man such as the one we described might look for a wife who will allow him to play the tyrant at the same time she mothers the child inside him. The woman we described would probably go out of her way to find a husband who will encourage her to play the submissive little wife who actually runs his life.

Emotionally, these people don't have well-developed sexual identities. They are uneasy about any feelings or fantasies that don't fit in with the more mature roles they have assumed. A man with doubts about his sexuality may feel like a ten-year-old wearing his father's pants. A sexually insecure woman may feel like a child wearing her mother's dress and noticing that she is flat-chested.

If such a man could accept his passivity, even his effeminacy, as parts of himself, there would be less of a gap between what he is and what he tries to be. If such a woman could live comfortably with her aggressiveness, there would be far less tension between her real and imagined needs. If such a couple got married and had children, the children themselves could accept this exchange of roles because their parents would be at ease in them. Perhaps the children would have a little trouble with children of other families, but that wouldn't be as confusing to them as the behavior of parents who try to be what they are not.

Instead there are couples trying to live down their sexual uncertainties, and at the same time trying to confirm them. In their marriages they must make uncomfortable compromises. For instance:

CECELIA AND KEITH

Very early in her life, when she was ten, Cecelia was seduced by an older man. Instead of frightening her, the experience pleased her, and she went back for more, again and again. Cecelia was discovering that she had strong sexual passions, and while they went against everything her parents had taught her, she seemed to have no control over them.

Eventually Cecelia's guilt began to fight against her sexual desires. The gap between her real and imagined needs became so wide that it was impossible for her to bridge the distance. She couldn't be a penitent and a whore at the same time. She did the next best thing as she saw it: she compromised. She married a man who punished her for her sins part of the time and then invited her to sin again.

Keith, her husband, is a man with nagging doubts about his potency. To cover up, he does everything he can to prove he is all man. Anything that hints

137

of gentleness infuriates him because it seems effeminate.

Keith keeps Cecelia tied down to a hard, dreary life. They have three children and a large house, all of which she must look after by herself. They could afford some domestic help, but Keith won't hear of it. He insists Cecelia must do all the work and do it well. If her dustcloth misses a spot, he finds it and complains.

In bed, however, Keith becomes a different person. This is where he allows himself to be what he really feels—passive, dependent, almost feminine in his need to know that he is attractive. Relying on his wife's more aggressive sexual behavior, he lies back and lets her make love to him. It is never the other way around.

Degrading Cecelia by day, needing her to seduce him by night, Keith provides at least some gratification to Cecelia's conflicting needs to express her passion, and then to be punished for it. In return, she allows him to take out on her the anger he feels toward his own dependent desires. When that anger is spent, and when those desires need reassurance, Cecelia is ready to give it.

PAM AND GREGORY

When he was in his teens, Gregory had several homosexual experiences with a few boys his age. He was rebelling against parents who were continually after him to perform, excel, and exceed. They were pushing him into manhood before he was ready for it, and he became convinced he would never make it. To satisfy his parents, he kept his grades up, but in his sex life he expressed his doubts that he was a man.

Gregory's mother was a castrating woman, and he developed both a fear and a resentment of all women. He did marry, and did love his wife, but he was unable to enjoy making love to her. Only rarely did he even try, and at those times he couldn't ejaculate. To him, an ejaculation meant that he was trying to destroy a woman by polluting her. Frightened by the intensity of his inner anger, he had learned to look upon women as asexual beings who simply couldn't arouse him.

Gregory no longer had any homosexual relationships, although he still had homosexual fantasies. This was his way of bringing other, stronger men down to his level so that he could be like them. He couldn't possibly fantasize about a sexual act with a woman because bringing her down to his level would mean that he and she were the same, and that's what he feared was true.

AUDREY AND MORT

Audrey came from a home where sexual identities were confused. Her mother was a harsh, bossy woman who acted like both father and mother to the girl. Her father was very meek with her mother, yet he slept with his daughter when she was only a child, stimulating her sensual appetites before she was able to control them. Audrey never really grew up. Inside she was still a child, still very much in need of a mother, yet compelled to prove that she was a woman. But the role of a woman was almost impossible for her to assume because it meant having a sexual relationship with a man, just as she had had with her father. She couldn't go through that, not again. The guilt she felt about her relationship with her father was too painful.

In a pitiful effort to juggle these conflicting needs, Audrey married a man who had been a homosexual earlier in his life and who still went cruising every now and then. She knew what he was, but he was what she wanted.

This marriage is in bad shape, but it continues to meet the needs of both husband and wife. By marrying, Audrey is proving to her mother that she is indeed a woman; in fact, a woman who can compete with her mother for the love of her father. By marrying a bisexual man, Audrey is also punishing herself for her sexual involvement with her father. She can also reassure herself that her man is all hers, for what other woman would want a bisexual man? But what about other men? Doesn't she have to compete with other men for her husband? Yes, she does, but to Audrey that isn't unusual or impossible. Her mother was so masculine that Audrey felt she was competing with a man when she won her father's affections away from her mother.

As much as she tries to be different, Audrey is becoming like her mother. She is domineering and forceful. She tries so hard to control her husband's life that she often drives him into homosexual affairs. But that, of course, assures her that she will continue to get what she needs from this marriage.

Who's who?

In a world where there is less and less difference between the things men and women do, it is hard for many
people to feel sure of who they are. Technological
changes have made it possible for men and women to do
the same kind of work, to drive the same kinds of cars,
to get the same kind of education, to live by the same
moral standards, to have equal sexual freedom, and to
compete with each other for the same world prizes. Very
rarely are they able to leave the stamp of their sexuality
on what they do. Very little in this world confirms what
they feel themselves to be.

In a successful marriage a man and woman can appreciate and confirm each other's sexual characteristics.
They can also appreciate and enhance each other's development as individuals. If a man enjoys his wife as a
woman, he'll enjoy seeing her use her talents, whether
she uses them as a homemaker or in a career outside the
home. A woman who enjoys her husband as a man will
welcome his interest in their home. While many things
in their life may change, he will approach new situations
as a man and she will approach them as a woman.

A husband and wife who are unsure of their masculinity and femininity have a totally different experience. On a conscious level their marriage is supposed to
eliminate their doubts, yet it is their unconscious doubts
that have brought them together. By giving each other
gratification for these repressed needs, they are also acknowledging each other's worst fears.

Because their unconscious desires are so repugnant to
them, these marriage partners rely very heavily on labels.
Going through the motions of "husband," "father,"

"man," "wife," "mother," "woman" maintains a protective distance between them and their fears. Not only one, but both partners must stick to their roles. A change in one cannot help but affect the appearance of the other, and appearance is what counts. With the motions becoming more and more the same for both sexes, the labels have less meaning. For instance, what difference does it make today if a woman wears pants more often than a skirt? It makes a frightening difference to a man who feels that pants make the man. And to a woman who feels that being in the kitchen makes her a woman, a man who fries an egg for himself may be a threat.

Does he or doesn't he?

In many of the marriages we described earlier in this book the partners had doubts about their sexuality. Doubt, then, is the real problem. If one or both of the partners was exclusively homosexual, the marriage wouldn't have taken place, or it would end, because a heterosexual relationship can't meet homosexual needs. These marriages took place because the partners *are* heterosexual, but they are confused about their sexual identities.

Certainly any marriage is vulnerable to change, but these sexually clouded marriages are especially threatened because sexual roles are changing faster than anything else in our society. Ironically, this is the area where these partners are weakest, yet this is where the greatest external pressure will be applied. To them, the social changes that are offering greater personal freedom and opportunity for expression to so many men and women will mean only that there is no place left to hide from their fears.

Sexual uncertainty

Many couples blame their marriage difficulties on other "sex problems." They may be very uncomfortable with each other because they are concerned about such things as impotence, frigidity, fear, or dislike of sex. They may, in fact, have chosen their mates to cover up these fears.

Sex rarely is a problem in itself. Usually it is a *symptom* of problems deep within the person. Therefore it makes very little sense for a couple to try to resolve their sex problems without probing further into their inner selves. Nor is it these sexual frustrations that create a gap within a marriage. The gap occurs only when a couple cannot be open and honest about their sexual difficulties and seek help with the problems causing them. Frigidity in a woman, for example, is caused not by marriage, but by the woman's earlier relationships with men and with her parents. Perhaps the answer lies in an irresponsible father who made it difficult for her to trust men. Impotency in a man also may be traced back to early pressures on a boy to take on the responsibilities of a man. In both cases inner tension frustrates the performance and enjoyment of the sex act. Similarly, a dislike or a fear of sex has roots in a person's relationships prior to marriage and is not caused by the marriage itself.

In marriages where the partners chose each other to satisfy or to cover up their sexual fears, there is no chance for them to discuss their problems with each other. One partner will often use the other's uncertainties as a weapon, but perhaps this is what the other partner really wants from the relationship. In this case, a gap is formed not by sex but by deeper problems.

Where there truly is a concern for the partner's welfare, as in more mature marriages, sexual tensions can be brought into the open. A woman who loves and trusts her husband can tell him, without fear of rejection or ridicule, that she simply can't seem to have an orgasm that night or that she is worried about a sex problem. Similarly, a man who is sure of his wife's affection can tell her that he gets up-tight when he tries to make love to her. Their next step is to do something about their problems, to find the help and self-understanding they need in order to enjoy a good sex life.

9

Children Caught in the Marriage Gap

Does it really matter if a husband and wife aren't aware of their unconscious needs as long as those needs are being met through the marriage? If a man and a woman are satisfied being miserable together—senseless though it may appear to others—what difference does it make? If the bumps on her head fit the holes in his, that's their business, right?

This is true if a couple's inner conflicts affect only themselves, but that rarely happens. If children are born to the marriage, they are the ones who must pay the price of their parents' inability to close the gap between their conscious and unconscious needs.

The scene is repeated every day in some psychotherapist's office: the tearful mother who can't understand why her child has become a vicious bully; the angry father who can't stand his "sissy" son; the proper parents of a foul-mouthed five-year-old; the calorie-counting parents of an obese daughter; plus the many under-achievers, drop-outs, liars, thieves, delinquents, drug addicts, and children with phobias, nightmares, and name-less fears.

As we mentioned earlier, children tend to act out the unfulfilled inner desires of their parents. In fact, the more the parents run away from their inner unconscious needs, the more likely they are to see them re-created in the behavior of their children. Parents who are in touch with their feelings can satisfy their own desires, leaving the child free to recognize his own.

Who told them?

A young mother whose ulcers "disappeared" soon after she became pregnant was horrified when her daughter developed ulcers at the age of eight months. Aware that she had been a "nervous wreck" before pregnancy but reluctant to probe into the cause of her conflicts, the young woman had convinced herself that she had been simply overeager to have a baby. When the ulcers disappeared, she was certain she was correct. But when her infant daughter began to repeat the pattern at such an early age the mother realized that her problem somehow had been communicated to the child.

"How?" she asked. "I don't even know what's bothering me! How can *she* know?" They were fair questions.

A gruff, extremely aggressive man refused to believe that his son was exhibiting his father's inner fears when he held back from sports or any activities that might have roughed him up. "I was a hockey player and a wrestler in college!" the father bellowed. "I've never been afraid of getting hurt! How would he get that kind of attitude from *me?*" It was a long time before he could acknowledge that behind his façade of the "strong man," he had serious doubts about his masculinity. His son, however, had picked up the signals immediately.

We cannot hide our inner needs from others as well as we may hide them from ourselves. They have a way of emerging through our attitudes, moods, tone of voice, facial expressions, gestures, and all the more subtle forms of communication between human beings. And children, whose senses are not yet dulled by all the sounds of our world, are especially receptive to what we really mean. The hug means nothing if the underlying feelings of the parent toward the child are hostility, jealousy, and resentment. Conversely, the child who is truly loved, consciously and unconsciously, knows it even if the parent doesn't always have time to demonstrate it.

Children "hear" what the parents feel rather than what they say. Thus the proper mother who has repressed her earlier desires to be promiscuous may influence her daughter to sleep around. The teetotaler father who can't admit that he'd really like to take a drink may be confronted by an alcoholic son.

Underlying the façade of many "devoted" parents who shower their children with material advantages, a home in the right neighborhood, good schools, a car, and the words "I love you" repeated regularly, there may be unsuspected forces that will shape a child's life—a cold, unresponsive father or one with a short-fused temper, a mother who is too headachey to face up to problems or a "crazy-clean" one who is preoccupied with the child's clothes and appearance. Regardless of the attempt to hide these forces, the child senses such things as sexual tensions between the parents or between parent and child. He takes as his own their guilts, real or imagined; their fantasied sins, long forgotten by them, become the child's. He knows that when his parasitic mother says,

"It's time for school, dear," she really means, "For God's sake, don't leave me—I can't live without you!" He pays no attention when his father says, "Stop looking like a bum and get your hair cut!" because he "hears" his father's repressed desire to rebel. Nonverbal as this parent-to-child communication process may be, it comes through loud and clear, with the parent saying, "Don't do as I say—do as I wish I could have done."

In order to win the parents' approval and avoid rejection, the child responds to the more powerful message. This becomes his image of himself, as he begins to repress his own inner needs and feelings.

Parents who don't have this gap within themselves usually can express what they truly feel. When they say something to a child, they back it up with their feelings, and the child senses that there is no conflict.

What do you want me to be?

The child of a couple who are out of touch with their inner feelings lives in painful confusion. Consciously his parents may be telling him one thing, but unconsciously they're sending another message. The child may pay little or no attention to the conscious demands because he senses that they aren't genuine, but when he obeys the unconscious suggestions he often shocks his parents by revealing their inner selves to them. He has done what they wanted him to do, become what they desired, yet here they are, screaming and shaking their fists in his face. How *dare* he! How *could* he! But, really—how could he not?

Consequently, we have a generation of long-haired,

casual, antimaterialistic sons and daughters rebelling against parents who conformed consciously, but unconsciously yearned to thumb their noses at the Establishment. On an individual basis as well, many young people are living out their parents' sexual tensions, hostilities toward their own parents, infantile fears, hatreds, and anxieties about themselves.

For instance:

JOE

Long before Joe was born, his mother succeeded in repressing her aggressive impulses and her envy of men. Now, however, they are reappearing in her relationship toward her son. To her conscious mind she is a devoted mother who never lets her boy out of her sight and allows no harm to come to him. Unconsciously, she's trying to castrate him. While Joe is encouraged to "be a real boy" and assert himself, he is not allowed to play rough games, or get dirty, ride a bicycle or go on hikes with his friends. Although he is seven, he is treated like a three-year-old.

Joe's father is a passive man who depends upon his wife to give him orders and make decisions for him. He can hardly help Joe to struggle against his mother's overwhelming protectiveness because he himself has submitted to it.

Gradually this child is giving in to the unconscious demands of his mother. In order to win her love and approval, he is beginning to deny his masculine needs and impulses and allow himself to be emasculated.

CARL

Carl's mother also had strong aggressive feelings that made her very uncomfortable. She denied that she was trying to castrate her son, just as she had castrated her husband, but to avoid feeling guilty about it, she unconsciously urged Carl to be a little bully. Carl's father, who saw his son as the young hero who could fight his battles for him, also encouraged the boy to be a "tough guy."

Carl, following the directions coming from the unconscious desires of both his parents, is now unable to get along with anyone his age. He is constantly fighting and arguing with his classmates and may be suspended from school. His mother and father are very upset about the boy's behavior, but no matter how severely they punish him, Carl knows he is doing exactly what they want. He is acting out his father's resentment toward his wife for overpowering him, and he is covering up the fact that his mother is now doing the same thing to him.

CAROL

Carol is an obese nine-year-old. Her mother takes her from doctor to doctor, seeking a "cure," but there seems to be none. Carol eats everything in sight.

Carol's mother, while slim, has an enormous appetite, which she has learned to control. But she has communicated her hunger to her daughter by talking constantly, hardly pausing for breath, and never giving the child a chance to say a word. To Carol, she was the big, open mouth ready to swallow the world (as compensation for the love she never got from *her* mother). Carol responded by opening her mouth—by biting, and eventually by cursing and shouting. Carol's playmates ran home bruised and bloody; their mothers complained, and Carol was punished.

Eventually Carol found a less painful way to satisfy her mother's hunger. She ate—and ate and ate. Her mother smiled and was quiet. She talked endlessly to others, but her conversation with Carol became normal, bearable. Even though she expressed concern about the child's weight, the food was always available. Carol herself has now become a big, open mouth ready to swallow the world.

What am I doing?

Children of parents who are able to express their inner feelings learn to respond in the same way. They say what they feel without anxiety, guilt, or apology. They are free to discover what is going on within themselves. They don't have to go through the hell of concluding that there is a difference between what they appear to be and what they really feel. Nor do they come to the painful decision that they must turn their backs on their inner beings, just as their parents have done. The smaller the gap within the parents, the smaller it is within the child.

Not all children of disturbed parents are afflicted in the same way. The child who best suits the parent's unconscious needs will feel the most pressure to act out those needs. The choice may depend upon such characteristics as the child's sex, place in the family, temperament, and physical appearance. The strength of the child's ego is another important factor: some children give in easily and some resist the parents' unconscious attempts to impose their own needs upon them. An unruly, rebellious child may in fact be fighting desperately to hang on to his own identity. For when a person denies his own needs and tries to live up to those of someone else, he becomes alienated from himself. A child senses this.

Some children submit, some rebel. Some appear to submit and instead withdraw into a fantasy world. In any case, they are deprived of the opportunity to mature, for in turning away from their own needs, their growth is arrested. What these children do is not of their own choosing, no matter how free their behavior appears to be. The gap is already being formed in a new generation.

Birthright

Children who come from broken homes or from parents with emotional problems have a hard time in their own intimate relationships. While there are some exceptions, many of these children do as their parents did in choosing a marriage partner: they seek out someone who can frustrate or satisfy their unconscious needs, and this in turn conflicts with the role they are playing. The gap begins all over again.

They have other disadvantages as well. Children of divorced or strife-torn parents tend to take on the defenses of the parent with whom they identify. The child of the mother who can't face difficulties and who runs out of the house slamming the door will probably do the same under similar circumstances. The father who can't work out his differences with his wife and keeps threatening divorce, may be teaching his child to do the same.

And then there is the very fact of divorce itself, showing a child that there is a ready way out of marriage if the going gets rough. Such a child, faced with the ordinary stresses and responsibilities of married life, may cut and run rather than attempt to resolve his differences with his partner. We are beginning to see this now in the attitudes of many young couples who are getting married, not forever, but "for as long as it lasts."

Perhaps the worst wound that warring parents can inflict on their children is to turn them against one of the parents. When divorce is accompanied by bitterness, guilt, blame, and the desire for revenge, it often happens that one parent tries to turn the child against the other. The child, who already is confused by the separation of the parents and may in fact feel—quite wrongly—that it was his fault, then begins to distrust not only his mother or his father, but all women or all men. Any future relationships formed by the child will certainly be distorted by these inner feelings.

A child deserves the opportunity to discover himself, to grow into the person he can be. He can do this if his parents are adults, if they are aware of what they want and need, if they are satisfying their own needs rather than depending on a child to do it for them—and if they are mature enough to respect the child's right to do the same.

His best chance for a good marriage—if this is what he chooses—is to have parents who are themselves happily married.

10

Seven Vital Dimensions
of a Good Marriage

A good marriage is more than one that "works out."
It is more than one that lasts only because its partners are
unable to reach out for something better in life. A good
marriage is alive. It grows. It offers a mature man and a
mature woman a life that is fuller, more productive, crea-
tive, satisfying, and rewarding than either could experience alone.

A good marriage is identifiable by the relationship of
the partners to each other. Its dimensions are: emotional
contact, freedom from defensiveness, freedom from
fear, flexibility, empathy, and a basic sense of independence with an ability to accept dependency.

Let's look at these dimensions one at a time:

Emotional contact

In a good marriage a husband and wife are aware of the inner feelings that each of them may arouse in the other, and they relate to them.

For instance:

KIM AND GORDON

This young couple have been married for six months. They both work, although neither of them earns a large salary because they are just starting out in their careers.

Kim would like their apartment to be more attractive when they entertain friends, but when she suggests buying more furniture, Gordon bristles. Kim's desire to spend money becomes a threat to him because they are going through a tight-money situation while they catch up on their bills. Gordon doesn't think their friends really care whether or not they have a lot of furniture, and he feels that his wife is making unfair demands on him.

Now, if Gordon were unable to face his own inner feelings, he might blow his top and accuse his wife of being selfish and extravagant, thereby creating a situation to which his wife couldn't respond because his charges wouldn't be true. Communication would then be cut off, and very likely new disagreements would arise out of this basic misunderstanding.

But Gordon is a mature person who can accept himself for what he is. Facing his resentment honestly, he finds that his wife touched off an emotion that already existed. He's a very careful budgeter who doesn't like being in debt, but he'd enjoy having a little more money to spend. He's also ambitious and wants to make more money, so he's a little sensitive about his position as a provider. Kim's remarks brought these inner feelings to the surface. Acknowledging this, Gordon is able to look at his wife objectively, realizing that perhaps she doesn't understand their money situation as well as he does. He explains it to her.

If Kim were less mature, she might pout and complain that Gordon wasn't giving her the kind of things her father gave her before she was married. She might also accuse him of opposing her just to spite her. Or she might threaten to use her own money for furniture instead of putting it into their household account.

But Kim is aware that Gordon is a responsible husband who doesn't like to spend their money recklessly. When she looks over their budget with him, she understands why they have to scrimp for the next few months. She agrees with Gordon that the new furniture can wait. They'll have just as much fun with their friends if they sit on the floor.

Or, Kim, in going over their budget, may see that the financial picture isn't as bleak as it appears to Gordon. She may realize that he is overreacting to his responsibilities as a husband and will be able to point that out to him. If this is so, Gordon will acknowledge his inner apprehension. Then they'll be able to go over the budget together, perhaps agreeing that they can afford one new piece of furniture now and get the rest later.

Because this couple are in touch with their inner feelings, they are able to verbalize them and make emotional contact with each other on the level where those feelings originate. It's only when couples try to cover up their deepest feelings that such contact becomes impossible because the emotion that is being expressed consciously —often in shouts and hostile accusations—is a substitute for the real thing. And if two people can't talk about what is actually on their minds, how can they make any sense to each other?

The ability to communicate on a deeper level makes it possible for some couples to handle situations that might disrupt marriages where there is less communication. For instance:

HOPE AND IRWIN

Irwin is a marketing analyst for a large corporation, and during the past ten years he has been transferred four times. This meant moving to a new part of the country, selling one house and buying another, packing, unpacking, leaving old friends and making new ones. Most of the burden fell on Hope's shoulders, but she always made the best of it. Now, however, with their three children in school, moving would be more difficult.

It happens again. Irwin comes home with the news that he is being transferred, and neither he nor Hope are happy about it. If they were to try to be "good sports" and put up a front for each other, they would be laying the groundwork for future hostile outbursts when the pressures of moving began to build up. They might, in fact, blame each other for what they were feeling but couldn't express, which would get them nowhere. Instead they face their own feelings and get them out in the open.

Hope says, "I wish we didn't have to move again. It's so nice here, and we have some wonderful friends. I sure hate to put the kids through the experience—they're doing so well in school."

Irwin agrees. "I'm tired of getting to know new places and new people. Besides, it interferes with my work. It's like starting a new job every couple of years."

Because they are able to express their displeasure without feeling guilty about it, this couple can look at their situation objectively. False emotions don't get in their way, because they don't feel they must live up to an unrealistic image of what a husband and wife "should" be. They may decide that moving is the price they must pay for a career that is worth the inconvenience. Perhaps all these transfers are the corporation's way of testing a man's capabilities for an administrative position, and this is what Irwin wants. In that case, the husband and wife will be able to help each other and their children as they go through the hardships of pulling up stakes.

Or, this couple may re-evaluate what Irwin is getting out of his work. If it isn't worth the sacrifices they must make, they may come to the decision that he should look for another job.

Freedom from defensiveness

In a good marriage the husband and wife can be their authentic selves. They know who they are, what they can do, and what they can't do. This means that they don't try to be more or less than what they are. They can admire and be proud of the capabilities of their mate without feeling that their own stature is diminished. They aren't defensive; neither are they compelled to compete with each other to prove one of them superior. Since they can accept themselves, they can accept each other.

For instance:

BERNICE AND LOU

When this couple began taking an art course two nights a week, it was immediately apparent that Bernice had an extraordinary talent for painting. Lou did well enough to enjoy the course, but he realized that his talent was on an amateur level.

An insecure, competitive couple might have been threatened by this situation. A husband who wanted to cover up unconscious feelings of inadequacy by trying to do everything perfectly might find his image damaged by a wife who displayed any abilities superior to his. A less mature wife who expected a husband to be an all-powerful, all-perfect, godlike figure might be uncomfortable when excelling him in anything.

Lou, however, is competent in many areas and he realistically accepts the fact that he can't do everything well. He appreciates Bernice's talent and encourages her to continue with her painting. When she completes her first canvas, Lou has it framed and displays it in their home. In the meantime, he continues to paint for the pure enjoyment of it as a hobby.

The ability to share

In a good marriage the husband and wife share in their abilities through their pride in each other. Instead of feeling that they must be identical, matching each other point for point with their accomplishments, they accept the fact that each will be outstanding in some areas in which the other is not.

For instance:

BERNICE AND LOU (CONTINUED)

Bernice is delighted with her newly discovered talent and plans to develop it. She is particularly pleased that Lou's admiration of her work gives them an opportunity to share their enjoyment of art. The experience also increases their ability to communicate with each other.

Bernice knows—and so does Lou—that his talents lie in other areas, and she is very proud of him. And because she knows what a pleasure it is to share in his accomplishments, she is glad to offer him a similar opportunity.

The ability of a couple to appreciate each other's accomplishments is especially important today when the traditional roles of husband and wife are changing. The husband who is aware of his own strengths and weaknesses won't be threatened by a wife who pursues a career, and the self-accepting wife won't feel displaced by a husband who knows his way around the kitchen.

Freedom from fear

In a good marriage the partners can accept their own and each other's limitations. They are not afraid of losing love, acceptance, or respect by bringing these limitations out in the open.

For instance:

BERNICE AND LOU (CONTINUED)

While it is quite true that Lou felt a twinge of jealousy when it first became apparent that Bernice was such a promising painter, he was able to bring his feeling to the surface. Looking over her shoulder at a still life she was doing, he said, "I sure wish I could paint that well."

It was an honest expression of his own limitations and Bernice accepted it that way. "You do very well," she told him, "and I'm glad you enjoy the course."

If Lou had been afraid to face his envious feelings and didn't allow himself to express them, they would have found their way to the surface sooner or later. Resentfully, he might have dropped out of the art course, and perhaps would have been critical of Bernice's work, trying to undermine her confidence in herself.

If Bernice had been unable to accept her own limitations in some areas of their life, she might have used her superior artistic talent as a weapon against her husband, especially if he were the kind who was reluctant to acknowledge the fact that his wife had any talent at all.

Flexibility

In a good marriage the husband and wife see each other as human beings, not as gods. They realize that there are some situations over which they have no control and to which they must bend.

For instance:

HOPE AND IRWIN (CONTINUED)

If this couple, faced with the prospect of the husband's transfer, could not accept each other as the persons they really are, their marriage might be in trouble. If Hope unrealistically assumed that her husband could avoid moving if he carried any weight in the corporation, or if she interpreted the transfer as an indication that her husband wasn't of much value to his employers, she might feel that he was letting her down. Eventually she would take out her resentment on him.

Similarly, if Irwin made unrealistic demands upon himself, feeling that he wouldn't be moved around if he were on a higher executive level, he might take out his hostility on his wife. Instead of using their energies to resolve the problem of whether or not to move, the couple would exhaust themselves by attacking each other for not being omnipotent.

Fortunately, Hope and Irwin can accept themselves and each other as human and therefore limited in their ability to control some of the situations in their lives. Hope realizes that Irwin is not the president of the corporation, nor can she expect him to be at the age of thirty-five. Irwin realizes that transfers are part of the company policy and that he must put up with them if he wants to get ahead.

Empathy

In a good marriage the husband and wife extend their flexibility to each other. They can "walk in each other's moccasins," accepting not only their own but each other's humanity.

For instance:

HOPE AND IRWIN (CONTINUED)

Both Hope and Irwin are aware that their apprehensions are related to the prospect of moving and not to any inadequacies in either of them. Irwin is striving to get ahead, to improve his family's way of life, and to develop his capabilities to their highest potential. Hope understands this. Because she can feel *with* her husband and realizes how important his goal is to him, she wants to work with him toward achieving it.

Irwin, on the other hand, is aware of the effort his wife is making. He is able to feel what she feels in giving up her friends and familiar surroundings, and he wants to help her as much as he can. He shares her concern over the adjustment their children will have to make and he works with his wife to help them understand why the move is necessary.

A basic sense of independence, with an ability to accept dependency

In a good marriage each partner is a whole person who is capable of making a life for himself or herself. Through the experience of marriage, each is willing and able to depend upon and cooperate with the other. Under certain situations, however, one will look to the other to act for him or her.

For instance:

HOPE AND IRWIN (CONTINUED)

In the past when they have moved, Irwin occasionally had to depend on Hope to close up their house while he went to take up his new duties in another part of the country. He was usually able to look for a house in that area, but Hope was left with the job of selling their former house and arranging for all their belongings to be packed, shipped, and stored. It was a difficult time for both of them, but they were able to get through it smoothly because each was able to act on his and her own as well as together.

Hope accepted the fact that Irwin couldn't be with her because he had other responsibilities that couldn't be set aside. In fact, she was pleased to pitch in and help, and she handled everything very well. If she had interpreted the situation unrealistically, resenting Irwin for "abandoning" her, or if she felt that she was burdened with a "man's" job, moving might have become a nightmare for both of them. Similarly, if Irwin imagined his wife to be a child who could do nothing on her own, he might have tried to handle everything himself, which would have been impossible. Unable to keep his mind on his work, resenting his wife for not helping him at the same time he was trying to keep her from lifting a finger, he would have been impossible to live with.

In this case, however, both husband and wife were able to support each other by acting out of their own strength when it was necessary.

As women move out into the world, it will become more important than ever that husbands and wives accept each other's need to have a life of his or her own. The woman who devotes her entire existence to her children is often left destitute when they grow up because she has no interests of her own upon which she can fall back—or better yet, with which she can move ahead. How often it happens that women in their middle years suffer severe depression because they expected their husbands to fill their lives just as the children once did, and of course they were disappointed. Many of these women married men who were uncomfortable whenever their wives showed any signs of strength or independence. Now, however, these same husbands complain that their wives "can't find some new interest in life."

When a husband and wife can accept each other's need for privacy and a life of his and her own—which in no way interferes with their ability to depend on each other—they will be able to adjust to the changes that occur in their lives as their children are born, as they grow, and as they leave the home. The wife will be able to accept the children's need to depend on her in their early years. Instead of resenting their demands upon her time and energy, she will enjoy the opportunity to care for their young needs, realizing that she is helping to prepare them for their own independence. If she's a working mother, she will arrange for someone to substitute for her during the hours she is away from them.

As the children grow, and as the wife has more time for herself, she will gradually develop her own interests and abilities so that when the children are no longer dependent upon her for their needs, she will be ready to move out into the world.

The husband, realizing that his wife needs other interests as much as he does, will encourage her to pursue them. He'll also accept her dependency on him. He won't simply turn over his paycheck and "leave the house to her." He will take an active interest in their home and in the upbringing of their children, giving his wife a hand whenever she needs one.

In their sexual relationship each partner in a good marriage is also able to be both dependent and depended upon. If the husband is occasionally aroused by something he reads, or by a picture or a remark, his wife doesn't rebuff him when he wants to make love to her. She doesn't object because he depends on her to satisfy his sexual needs. Nor does she say, "You don't want me for myself, you only want my body!" She realizes that she isn't the only source of sexual stimulation in the world and she enjoys their sex life as much as her husband does.

The husband also acknowledges his wife's ability to become independently aroused. He doesn't feel that she should be aroused only by him and only when he pleases. He doesn't complain that his wife is "aggressive." Like her, he enjoys sharing in the satisfaction of her needs.

Together, this couple delight in their deepening sexual experience with each other rather than bickering over who made the advances and why. They accept each one's need for the other. They realize that in each one's life there is an area that is private, because each is an individual, but that their marriage enables them to help each other work off the tensions that arise in these unconscious levels of their beings.

What holds the dimensions together?

In a good marriage, these seven vital dimensions are present. The partners are aware of their conscious and unconscious needs, and there is no serious conflict between these needs. They have become familiar with their inner desires and emotions by paying attention to the clues that emerge, however fleetingly, from their feelings and thoughts. They are people who can face themselves. They also express what they are without shame, apology, or fear. Consequently, there is no wide gap between what they feel and what they communicate, either openly or subtly.

For the most part, the smaller the gap between the conscious and unconscious needs of the individuals, the smaller the gap in their marriage. Their apparent marriage contract is congruent with their hidden contract. They can work together smoothly, lovingly, and in all the dimensions necessary to make a good life for both of them.

PART IV

FACING THE TRUTH: WHAT CAN YOU DO ABOUT A DYING MARRIAGE?

11

Can Breaking Marriages
Be Saved?

Good marriages are the exception today. The marriages we hear more about—because there are more of them—are the ones that are coming apart. More couples are changing partners or going their separate ways; fewer who start out together are continuing that way. Perhaps the most surprising breakups are marriages that have lasted twenty years or more.

Why? That's what everyone wants to know when a marriage comes apart. Why? Was it another man? Another woman? Not enough money? Too much? Was it because the couple didn't have children? Or because they did? Was it an obsession with a career? Or the inability to hold onto a job? What happened to make two people stop needing each other? And can it happen to *any* marriage?

Marriage is a tough, binding relationship. It can survive the most miserable circumstances and the most catastrophic events. While infidelity, deprivation, extravagance, the presence of unwanted children, the absence of very-much-wanted children, and various forms of insecurity may be hard to bear, they usually don't destroy a marriage. Quite often, because they may fulfill the unconscious desires of a husband and wife, they hold a marriage together.

But today marriage is under heavy pressure from within and without. People are less sure of who and what they are, and of what they want out of life. Instead of trying to learn who we really are, we are trying on different life-styles that are poorly designed for human wear. The roles of man and woman are changing, our living space is getting smaller, occupations are becoming obsolete almost before we can master them, the size of our families is shrinking. What we see around us today may be gone or replaced tomorrow.

Change isn't an isolated phenomenon. People react to it. If something is different in one area of our life, other areas will be affected. We may fight the change, embrace it, or try to ignore it, but we can't remain the same. Neither can a marriage. That's why a man and woman have to be flexible if their marriage is to survive.

As long as a husband and wife are getting what they need from each other, their marriage is likely to remain intact. It doesn't matter whether their basic needs are ordinary or bizarre, conscious or unconscious. If a woman is satisfied with a man who wakes her at three o'clock in the morning and beats the hell out of her, and if he's getting what he wants by doing it, their marriage is working for them. It may be a pretty sick relationship, but it's not about to end unless she gets tired of bruises or he finds it possible to sleep through the night.

In other words, marriages end when one or both partners can't, or won't, continue to satisfy the other's needs.

No matter how well they may suit each other in the beginning of their marriage, a husband and wife can't count on staying in that fixed position. Human needs don't always remain the same.

As we grow older, as we experience more of life, as our world changes, we change, too. We don't always require the same things. We become aware of new desires, new hungers, and we want different experiences from our relationships. As our new needs are fulfilled, they give birth to still newer needs. This is one of the ways in which we mature.

Flexible, adult husbands and wives who are in touch with their own feelings are also sensitive to the changing needs in the other. Because they are fully developed people, their new desires grow out of their basic needs. They evolve. As these new needs become known, the partners are free to search themselves for ways to fulfill them. As they discover new qualities in themselves, they change still more. That's because they're not afraid of newness. Growth is a part of their life, and they welcome it. As the husband and wife grow individually, they also grow closer together because their mutual satisfaction in each other is that much deeper.

These couples are less likely to be confused by the variety of life-styles available today. Because they know who they are and what they want, they can allow their needs to choose what is right for them. If they make a poor choice, they will probably realize it quickly and be able to change direction. While the rapid pace and tension of life today may at times distract and irritate them, it won't tear them apart. At the center of their beings they are intact.

It's the less mature couple who are painfully vulnerable to the ravages of change. They, who want so desperately to remain the same, are far more likely to react traumatically to changes as they grow older. Instead of evolving gradually, change, for these people, may come as a sudden leap into another level of life for which the rest of the personality is poorly prepared. What was satisfying at a previous level of life may become totally unwanted. New desires may have little or nothing to do with former ones. And because the mate was chosen to gratify earlier childish needs, he or she may not be able to fulfill them at another level of life. For instance:

DENISE AND VINCENT

Denise was a good wife in many ways, and in their earlier years together Vincent needed her to mother him. Now, however, his needs were changing. He expressed them by objecting to the way Denise was bringing up their two sons. He felt she coddled them too much, yet when Vincent complained about it, Denise murmured, "Yes, dear," and did exactly as she pleased.

Denise couldn't see that Vincent was changing with age. As he matured he needed less mothering; he was ready to be more of a man, and he wanted his wife to respond to him on that level. While he wasn't strong enough to stand up against his wife, he began to seek a more satisfying way of life. Eventually he found it with a woman who worked in his office.

Denise was shocked when Vincent asked for a divorce. She hadn't seen it coming, but even if she had she would have been incapable of fulfilling her husband's emerging desires.

Very rarely will two people grow at the same time and at the same pace. If there is growth at all, usually one partner outdistances the other, and unless they try to relate to each other, one of them may look for satisfaction somewhere else.

It's hard for some people to realize that they or their partners are changing. Because they're so afraid of anything new, they try to ignore it until it disrupts their lives. And because they don't permit their feelings to influence their conscious behavior, they can conceal their new desires from themselves and their mates for a long time.

For instance:

EILEEN AND ROY

Eileen needed a man she could call her own, and that's what she thought she had in Roy. For the first few years of their marriage, she had no reason to complain, and then Roy began to stray. Finally he had an affair, but when Eileen found out about it, he said he had no intention of giving up the other woman. He wanted to keep her and his wife as well. In fact, he was surprised when Eileen left him.

It's easy to blame the failure of this marriage on infidelity, but that isn't what really happened. The reason why Eileen left her husband was that he no longer satisfied her need to possess and be possessed. Roy, however, didn't even realize that his needs had changed, making him incapable of giving Eileen what she expected from their marriage.

Even if a couple doesn't grow at all, they can't avoid being influenced by a changing world. A man who feels like a boy and a woman who feels like a little girl will be deeply upset by the changes in male and female roles in our society. They will feel as if their identity is changing along with them, yet in their actions they will often go along with the changes because they think these are the things they must do to prove they are adults. This can be a terrible strain on two people bound together by unconscious needs they cannot face.

The missing piece

It's only natural that people want to know how to put a marriage back together after it comes apart. A lot of hopes, a lot of time and energy, a lot of living go into this most intimate relationship, and couples don't want to sacrifice this. What they want is a simple formula for a happily married life.

Unfortunately, the chances for repairing a broken marriage are very slim. You can't put something back together when you don't have all the pieces, and this is what happens when a marriage breaks down. Something has gone out of it. Something that was needed to hold it together is no longer there, and usually it can't be replaced. Bringing the partners back together would be like introducing two strangers to each other: there is little to hold them together. They would have to find new forms of satisfaction in each other before they could resume their life together, and their marriage would be quite different from what it was. Only rarely could this possibly happen.

The reasons for marital failures lie deep within the individual husband and wife. Discovering what these reasons are and learning something from them takes more time and self-examination than most couples are willing to endure. Many men and women find this an especially painful procedure because it means that they must face the very thing they want to avoid: themselves. It's easier, for the time being, to blame the marriage itself or a partner or the way of the world. It's easier to go on making the same mistakes over and over and over. This is what happens to people who don't know what they need out of life.

It takes two

Just as it takes two people with interacting needs to begin a marriage, it takes two with conflicting needs to end one. The breakdown of a marriage is never one partner's fault, even if it is only one partner whose needs have changed. The one who hasn't changed is just as much a cause of their mutual inability to gratify each other. That's why a dying marriage can't be resuscitated by only one spouse. For instance:

STEPHANIE AND BEN

When Stephanie married Ben, she had such a poor image of herself that she overlooked his some-what sadistic tendencies. She was grateful to be wanted by a man, and Ben's abusive behavior was no worse than the treatment Stephanie had known from her parents.

Ben never did anything to please his wife. He never took her out or encouraged her to invite her friends to their home. He was an antisocial man with few friends of his own, and he couldn't understand why his wife sometimes felt lonely being at home all day.

Stephanie was a good wife who worked very hard keeping up their home and caring for their son and daughter. She could never win a word of praise from Ben no matter what she did, but she seemed satisfied with her life. However, when their daughter began to experience severe emotional problems, Ben and Stephanie followed the advice of the high-school counselor and took the girl to a psychotherapist. During the course of several preliminary interviews between the parents and the psychotherapist Stephanie began to take another look at herself. She saw that she was a decent, warm, intelligent woman who deserved far better treatment than she had received from her parents and her husband. At first this discovery delighted her and made her want to learn more about her potential, so she asked the psychotherapist if she could consult him as a patient. He agreed, and Stephanie saw him three times before Ben began to complain about the change that was "coming over her." He wanted her exactly the way she had been, because she fulfilled his need to express his hostility toward women. He threatened to leave his wife if she didn't stop seeing the psychotherapist.

During her next consultation Stephanie considered the possibility that her own development might cost her her marriage. It was a price she couldn't pay, at least at that time, and she withdrew from psychotherapy.

Having gained a little self-respect, Stephanie was no longer the subservient wife she had once been.

But because she knew she lacked the confidence to look for a better way of life, she accepted the bargain she had made with Ben. He was still an abusive, neglectful husband, but Stephanie realized that she couldn't expect him to be different simply because she had changed. In an effort to find more satisfaction in other areas of her life, Stephanie began to see her friends more often, and with them she managed to do some things she never did with her husband. With whatever money she could eke out of her household allowance she bought tickets to plays and concerts. She took a few courses at a community college and became active in an amateur theater group. Most of these things she did during the day, and by late afternoon she was always home preparing dinner and ready for Ben's return. Her evenings were quiet and frustrating, but she found them tolerable because her days were so interesting. All in all, Stephanie felt she had worked out a pretty good compromise between her own needs and her husband's.

Stephanie did the best she could at the time, but her compromise is on shaky ground. She may gain more confidence in herself as she becomes more active with other people. Eventually she may begin to rebel against a husband who still sees her as an inferior, insensitive creature. And suppose she meets a man who responds to her needs to be loved and appreciated? In other words, Stephanie may continue to change in spite of herself. Because she is aware that her emerging needs are disturbing her relationship with her husband, she may be able to repress them and prolong the life of her marriage, but she can't guarantee it.

Ben, too, may begin to sense that he is not getting what he needs from his wife. The fact that Stephanie is patient and submissive may not always be enough for him. Part of his satisfaction came from fulfilling *her* need to be abused, and that is no longer part of their relationship.

What if Ben were to realize that he was partially responsible for the frustration he is beginning to feel? What if he also began to search himself in an honest effort to understand what he wants out of life? Would his marriage have a better chance for survival?

The answer to the last question is both Yes and No. Any marriage is helped when a husband and wife can understand what they are really asking from each other and what they may be refusing to give. When their needs are out in the open, it's easier for them to see where the frustration lies. Blaming things, events, circumstances, or other people makes no sense. Any readjustment must take place between *themselves* as individuals.

The best hope for saving a failing marriage lies in the possibility that each partner will be able to face his and her innermost needs. If they can come to a better understanding of themselves, they may be able to reduce the gap between what they are and what they think they are. Perhaps, through some insight into whatever handicapped their individual growth at an earlier age, they may begin to mature as persons. While this doesn't automatically insure that one partner's needs will again mesh with the needs of the other, there is at least a possibility that this may happen.

Sometimes, when a husband and a wife gain some insight into themselves, they find new meaning in their marriage. But very often one or both partners find that their self-understanding makes their marriage intolerable. Even in the case of a marriage that comes to an end *because* the partners finally realize that they cannot satisfy each other's needs, however, each of these two people will have an opportunity to find happiness with someone else. It may hurt them to grow, but through that growth they will develop a much more rewarding way of life.

Make it better—fast

The future for many marriages would be brighter if frustrated couples could simply go to a psychotherapist and find out what's bothering them. But we human beings are far more complicated than that, and so are our relationships. No two marriages are alike, just as no two individuals are alike. Our unique, personal characteristics give a distinct color to our relationships, which makes a readjustment of needs very difficult to achieve. A pat solution won't do. The solution has to be individualized.

In the first place, not everyone wants to know his own needs. People who have spent a lifetime hiding from themselves aren't going to rush into self-discovery. Many fight it. Some will refuse and back away. And if some have managed to get along even fairly well behind a façade, they may not agree that they should come out from behind it. Why not try the same façade in a new setting and with a new partner? To get something out of psychotherapy a person has to go into it with a certain amount of self-awareness—or at least the desire for it.

In the second place, psychotherapy is a long, expensive procedure that not everybody can endure or afford.

If a person is strongly motivated by his own desire to understand himself, he finds the experience worthwhile. If he is undergoing it because his spouse says he should, or because she's seeing a psychotherapist, too, or because it's the thing to do, he may not get enough out of his sessions to encourage him to continue.

Psychotherapy involves a process of becoming aware of one's self. As a person begins to realize what he really feels and needs, the gap between his desires and his behavior begins to close. This is an oversimplification, but as a person retraces his emotional steps back to the place where his growth was arrested, usually he can begin to identify the desires he has been repressing. Gradually, as he is able to remove the obstacles that were once in his way, he will grow through those levels he has missed and become an adult. Then there will be nothing to hide and no need for games. What you'll see is what he is.

If a person can benefit from psychotherapy, he changes, but the change comes from within, from his feelings on out to his actions. This is one of the reasons why the procedure takes so long. It means that a person understands what he is doing when he is doing it. And because his actions proceed from his innermost needs, his behavior will be more consistent. He will also be more confident about meeting new, spontaneous situations because he knows he can rely on his needs and desires to guide him. This self-knowledge may take a long time to acquire, but it is far-reaching and lasting.

Today, however, many people are in too much of a hurry to undergo psychotherapy. If there's a pain in their life, they want it alleviated instantly. If there were a pill or an exercise or a prayer that would end frustration, it would become an overnight sensation.

In this age of computerization, we also tend to see ourselves as pieces of electronic machinery into which happiness can be programmed. Why not? Why not dial-a-solution to our problems? If we're doing something wrong, why not find out what is right and *do* it? If our mates jump down our throats every time we open our mouths, why not learn to say something more pleasing? Never mind changing from the inside out. Let's get to what's on the outside and change *that*. This, in a sense, is what the behavior therapists are saying. Their views represent a relatively new school of thought that is more concerned with *what* people do than with *why* they do it. Their conviction is that the *why* is not important (as the Freudians think), that it takes too much time to unravel the *why* and to produce the kind of results that change lives. The behaviorists have a *now* philosophy about human existence. They feel that by consciously changing what we do we can improve the way we live, quickly and obviously. If we want to be happy, we can make ourselves do those things that will make us happy.

In a society where people are losing touch with their feelings, the behavior-therapy approach to human problems has great appeal. It fits into the currently popular belief that we must act first, then feel. By taking this philosophy a step further, it offers us the hope that if we want to experience a certain feeling, we can achieve it by performing certain actions. If we want to feel love, we must do things that are kind, thoughtful, affectionate. If we want to get over our shyness, we must begin to talk to other people. If we can't think of a thing to say, there are endless varieties of topical lists and suggested dialogue to guide us.

Healing the deeper wounds

Marriages don't end overnight. While the final breakup may be abrupt and occasionally explosive, the causes of separation were formed over a long period of time. They began before the marriage began, in the lives of the two individuals who came together. Men and women can't expect to understand them or to change them in an instant. Yet that's what they are trying to do when they ask for quick, superficial solutions to their marital problems.

Changing the way people behave doesn't change the way they feel. Saying different words, using new gestures, throwing themselves into untried activities, doesn't alter their basic needs. They will continue to demand satisfaction on either a conscious or an unconscious level.

The trend, however, is away from an intense, inner exploration of the self. As the need for self-understanding becomes more urgent, as the lack of it disrupts an alarming number of lives, men and women are turning toward the new therapies that seek to change *what* they do and *how* they do it.

It will be many years before we can evaluate the results of these new therapies. While at first they may have seemed simplistic in their approach to human relationships, it is becoming apparent that they are helping some people with their problems. Undoubtedly there is a need and a place for them in our fast-paced society. The questions we should consider are, Who are the people they can help? And what kind of help do they offer?

12

Trying the New Therapies

One of man's most painful needs today is to be in close touch with another human being. Cut off as we are from ourselves, we are also cut off from each other. No matter how closely we live with another person, we may feel isolated, out of reach, unable to touch and be touched.

Contact, touch, interaction with other human beings—these, above all else, are what the new therapies offer. To people with problems they can't identify, much less understand and resolve, contact is vital. The touch of a hand, the warmth of another person's skin under one's fingers, being passed bodily from one member of a group to the next, being lifted into the air and kept from falling only by the arms of those holding you—these are the things that tell you someone knows you're alive if you are so cut off from your feelings that you have no other way of realizing it. These gestures confirm the fact that you are not a machine, but human.

How they work

Psychoanalytic forms of therapy are lonely experiences. Even though the patient works through his problems with the help of a psychotherapist, the very purpose of the procedure is to enable the patient to find himself, to mature. Only he can do that. No one else can feel his frustrations for him; no one else can probe his way through them to more adult levels of life. No one else is quite like him. Even if the therapist were to present the patient with a version of what he is, it would be an inaccurate, edited statement of himself. He and he alone can discover his own authenticity. He can be guided and perhaps kept from straying off into detours, but no one can hold his hand or give him sympathy.

In the classic form of analytical group therapy, which is an extension of individual analysis, the person is also on his own. He explores his reactions and interactions with other people to see what makes *him* tick. By himself he must work his way into or out of the group.

The encounter group is a totally different experience. The new member immediately finds companionship, sympathetic attention to his problems and acceptance in spite of them. He doesn't have to develop into an attractive person; he is welcome because he *is* a person. From there, he works with the group to eliminate or change the forms of behavior that are leading to frustration. He raps with the group and learns from them what it is about him that gets their backs up. He reciprocates by telling them how they bug him. Everyone lets his hair down, and that, undeniably, is a delicious sensation of release in itself.

Loosening up may take anywhere from a marathon weekend to several months, but in any case it is much faster than classical forms of psychotherapy. And there *are* results. Many people come away from these meetings feeling much better than when they arrived. The sense of companionship, the opportunity to talk out one's anxieties, the realization that there are others with problems, and, with luck, the discovery that the obstacles to a productive life lie within the self, and therefore within one's ability to alter, are encouraging.

People with uncomplicated problems—for instance, those who are bored, or those who want a change of scene to get them out of a rut—may require nothing more than a good encounter group. But the person with deep inner conflicts needs much more. For this person, the release, the optimism, the feeling of acceptance he gets from the group will not last. His life will still be dominated by his unsatisfied, repressed desires, and a deliberate change in his behavior becomes merely a revised facade. The best thing he can get out of an encounter group is the realization that he needs more help. Sometimes this happens.

For instance:

NICK

On his own, Nick probably wouldn't have gone to a therapist. He didn't really think he needed one. He was pleased with his life. He was a well-paid, well-performing executive for a large corporation, and he had every reason to expect that he would reach the top of the administrative ladder within a few more years. His wife was still with him and his three kids were doing well in school. He didn't have any close friends, but he didn't mind because he had so little time for socializing. And what if some of his colleagues didn't like him? As long as they respected him, that was what counted.

When the personnel manager of Nick's company sent a memo to all executives inviting them to an encounter-type seminar on business relationships, Nick attended it just to be a good sport. Actually he thought it would be a waste of time.

The seminar was quite different from anything Nick expected. Instead of discussing the usual range of topics such as motivating a staff, presenting ideas with conviction, and finding new inspiration from old routines, the group leader encouraged the executives to discuss how they felt about their coworkers, their superiors, their employees, and themselves. Quite suddenly Nick began to see things in his attitude that were far from the image he had carefully presented to others over the years. He saw that his colleagues had some reasons to dislike him. He was ruthless, unconcerned for their feelings, and jealous of their abilities. When he extended his insights into his home life, he realized that he was a sadistic husband and a hypercritical father.

When the seminar ended, Nick was preoccupied with what he had learned. He realized he had been hiding behind his business success; now he wanted to be more of a person. Because he decided he needed something besides a change in his behavior, Nick began to consult a psychotherapist. Eventually his behavior did change, but it was the result of his development on the deeper levels of his personality.

Where does it hurt?

Many of the new therapies are useful in their way.
What we get from them depends upon how we use them.
Talking out their feelings in the group and exploring the
reactions to what is said may be helpful to some people,
unless their feelings are expressions of very deep-seated
conflicts. In that case, a deliberate change in their behavior will only delay or prevent the discovery of their real
needs and fears. For example, a woman who is frigid may
go to a sexual-behavior clinic and learn how to experience an orgasm, but that doesn't mean she isn't frigid
anymore. It may mean that she is now a frigid woman
who can have an orgasm. Because her frigidity per-
meated far more than the physiosexual area of her life,
it will take more than a behavioristic change to relieve
her inner frustration.

When it comes to exploring marital difficulties, the
new therapies tend to treat the marriage instead of the
individuals involved in it. Many of the recent books on
marriage and other intimate human relationships are
little more than attempts to put words in people's
mouths. In certain situations we are supposed to say
certain things to bring about—or to avoid—certain responses. This approach is based on the assumption that
people want to communicate. But what about those who
want to argue, to criticize, to withdraw into a punishing
silence, or to be abused? No matter how carefully these
people used prescribed words and various forms of body
language, they will still have the same basic motivations
and they will find a way to express them.

Unfortunately, the new therapies also provide an easy
out for people who don't really want to face themselves.
Some of the most troubled men and women go from one

group to another, loudly proclaiming how good they feel, but learning nothing about what they feel.

For instance:

RHODA AND DENNIS

Rhoda and Dennis were becoming an uptight couple and didn't know why. They had begun to bicker a lot, never seriously, but enough to make them uncomfortable with each other. Dennis was working later and later at the office because he didn't enjoy being home, and Rhoda was trying to get her mind off her problems by throwing herself into as many activities as she could find. Eventually she became involved in an encounter program and felt so elated after a few meetings that she talked Dennis into going with her. After one meeting he was convinced that his only problem was a reluctance to loosen up, to say what was on his mind and to confront his hostilities toward others, especially toward his wife. He thought the group could help him become more relaxed.

Within a few weeks Rhoda and Dennis became so wrapped up in the group that there was hardly time for anything else in their lives. Finally Dennis gave up his job and they sold their house so they could live with a group that was forming in another part of the country.

During this time their behavior changed radically. Instead of being shy with other people, they were now among the more aggressive members of the group. Rhoda was the first to experiment sexually outside their marriage, but Dennis quickly followed her example. From there they went on to group sex.

They were stimulated by their experiences, but their relationship as husband and wife had deteriorated to the point where they could no longer live together. Each of them went his separate way, living with various members of the group for short periods of time, and eventually they were divorced. Neither one has since been able to live with another partner for more than a few months at a time.

It's obvious that these two people were using their encounter therapies as an escape from their real problems. In spite of the massive changes they made in their way of life, they never even approached an understanding of their basic needs. Beneath the altered surface of their personalities they were the same frustrated human beings who were outgrowing their ability to satisfy each other. Whatever broke up their marriage was now making it impossible for either of them to achieve a lasting relationship with anyone else—but it's still a mystery to them.

While this is an extreme example of what can go wrong in therapy groups, there are other hazards. The group leaders are not required to have a license of any kind, nor must they undergo any special training for their work. While many of them are skilled professionals, well-trained in psychological methods—and some are practicing psychiatrists and psychologists—they do not *have* to be. *Anyone* can lead a group.

Professional training doesn't guarantee that a group leader will be effective. As many people are aware, there are good and bad qualified professional therapists, and credentials aren't a guarantee of talent and skill. Nevertheless, training does alert the therapist to the fact that he is dealing with something volatile when he attempts to explore human emotions. Too often the person who is on the brink of emotional collapse can go undetected by an untrained group leader. Too often the symptoms of severe depression are not spotted in time. The group raps, personalities clash, anxieties are exposed—and some people come apart under the pressure. Sometimes the ego must be built up before the self can be revealed, and this is a job for the experienced psychotherapist.

Where the help is needed

Encounter groups and marriage counseling may help to smooth out some of the wrinkles on the surface of a person and give more color to his life. But for those who need to grow and to close the gap between what they are and what they're going to be, encouraging them to behave differently only perpetuates their self-deception.

Broken marriages are caused by people who are poorly equipped to deal with life as it is. That's why it does no good to try to put a marriage back together without first aiding the people involved. These people *are* lonely. They do need to make contact with themselves and with each other. Their increasing frustration and their inability to form intimate relationships are symptoms of their confusion over what they want from life. Changing their life-styles treats the symptoms but leaves the problems crying out for attention. What these people need more than any kind of therapy, new or old, is the encouragement to grow, to face their needs without fear and guilt so they can choose a life partner who will meet those needs, and to mature along with them.

13

When It's Time to Uncouple

A divorce attorney recently commented that most of his clients make this statement once they've begun divorce proceedings: "I only wish I had done it sooner."

Getting to that point, however, is a painful journey for many men and women. They are confused by feelings of rejection, shock, anger, guilt over leaving a partner and perhaps their children, fears about getting along on their own and apprehensions about bringing up children in a one-parent home. Add to that their concern for the opinions of relatives and friends and it is understandable why divorce is a difficult action to take.

"If only I could just walk out and call it finished," said a young woman who wanted to end her marriage but just couldn't bring herself to consult an attorney.

"My wife's the dependent kind," a middle-aged man said. "I can't tell her that it's all over between us. Not just yet. I don't know what she'll do without me."

"If I leave my wife, I have to leave my kids," said a young husband. "How can I do that?"

"I keep wondering where I'll go—how I'll live," said a mother of three small children. "My children are too young to live with a stranger, and I don't have a family to go back to."

"The things you have to go through to get a divorce!" complained a man who has wanted to end his marriage for a long time. "My wife and I don't hate each other— we just don't do anything for each other. Yet, to get a divorce one of us has to play the monster and the other one the victim."

"My husband's an alcoholic," said a woman married fifteen years. "I know there's no hope for our marriage, but I feel so rotten every time I think about leaving him."

Nevertheless, divorce is, under certain circumstances, an advisable step for some couples to take. Prolonging a marriage that is destructive to one or both partners is senseless, cruel, and unrealistic. And if a marriage is not meeting the basic emotional needs of one or both partners, it is already dead, in a psychological sense. Divorce is merely the legal acknowledgment of this fact.

In these "certain circumstances," the marriage gap has become so vast that the partners can no longer span the distance between their conscious and unconscious needs. One or both will be hurt by continuing the relationship; at the very least, growth for either one becomes impossible. Rather than fulfilling each other's needs, however immature they may have been, the partners in these marriages are in the position of satisfying one and frustrating the other.

And what are these circumstances?

When one partner satisfies his or her needs at the expense of the other

In many marriages one partner attempts to increase his or her stature by stepping on the neck of the other. If this is their unconscious agreement, they're both getting satisfaction out of their relationship. But when one partner gets tired of being abused, that's the end of the mutual exchange and the beginning of hurt.

For instance:

AMY AND BOB

Earlier in her life, Amy's deep need for affection and approval led her into several affairs. They ended badly, and in two instances she had an abortion, which left her with the fear that she was unable to control her behavior. She married a man who could do it for her.

During the first three years of their marriage Amy was content to allow Bob to dominate her, criticize her, and subject her to ridicule in front of their friends. Her husband's abusive treatment confirmed her own contemptuous image of herself and provided the emotional restraints she felt she lacked.

Bob was an insecure man who resented Amy's family background because he believed it was superior to his own. But he needed a wife like Amy to help him cover up his sense of inadequacy. By belittling her, especially in the presence of other people, he felt bigger, stronger, and more powerful than he really was.

The marriage worked until Amy, through more frequent contact with her friends, began to realize that they respected her far more than her husband did. She gained a little more self-esteem in her job as a librarian when her new storytelling program for children was approved with enthusiasm by both parents and children.

Bob, however, was unable to accept Amy's improved image of herself because it conflicted with his unconscious need to demean her. The more confidence she gained, the more he ridiculed her, until finally the marriage became unbearable for her.

It took a long time for Amy to leave Bob and get a divorce, but once she did she found that she had matured quite a bit during the years. Because she was more comfortable with herself and able to express her needs more openly, she was not driven to seek approval in meaningless affairs. As her guilt feelings about her past subsided, she also found that now she was able to control her behavior and was less likely to do things that conflicted with her real needs.

When a marriage can no longer serve the needs of both partners, when one partner's self-confidence must be crushed in order to build up the other's ego, that marriage is already ended. Through separation and divorce at least one of the partners may gain the opportunity to work toward a better, more satisfying way of life.

When one partner is so abusive that he or she threatens the well-being of the other

In some sado-masochistic marriages the couples act out what might be called "The Bavarian Clock Syndrome." Every hour on the hour one spouse comes out and hits the other on the head, knowing very well that the next hour the other will retaliate.

For instance:

JANET AND BRUCE

Bruce was a heavy drinker who took out his frustration on his wife. When he came home drunk, he beat her, and once he broke her nose. She retaliated by calling the police and having him arrested.

For twenty years this marriage went on, in spite of friends and relatives who urged them to end it, because both Bruce and Janet needed what they were getting from the other. He could express his hostility toward his mother by abusing his wife, and she could gratify her contempt for men by provoking her husband into losing his control of himself, even if she got hurt in the process.

To cover up their inner need for each other, this couple frequently sought the advice of a marriage counselor, none of which they followed. Janet, however, went into group psychotherapy and there she began to gain some insight into herself. Finally she was able to see how devastating her marriage was, and when Bruce refused to seek any help for his problems, Janet decided on a divorce.

This marriage really ended when the wife no longer needed to feed her contempt for her husband. Simultaneously she became incapable of satisfying her husband's need to hurt and humiliate her. Prolonging the marriage would have meant that the wife had to sacrifice herself—and her opportunity to grow into a productive person—in order to fulfill the husband's sadistic appetites. Under their changed circumstances that would have been impossible.

When one partner grows and the other either cannot or will not

In a marriage where both partners can develop and adapt to the changes in each other the relationship deepens and becomes more satisfying. However, when one of the partners grows while the other stays in the same old rut, problems ensue.

For instance:

SHARON AND TED

Early in their marriage, Ted was very happy to become a part of Sharon's family. They were warm, generous people who "adopted" him as one of their own. For Ted, who had been brought up by aloof, undemonstrative parents, this was exactly what he wanted. Before long he and Sharon moved in with her family and were totally absorbed in their close-knit way of life. They ate together, went on vacations together, and had the same friends.

As Ted's job called upon him to travel to different parts of the country, he began to see that there was

more to life than the narrow little world he and
Sharon shared with her parents. He thought it
would do Sharon good to travel with him, but whenever he invited her along, she found an excuse to
stay home. Eventually, through meeting different
kinds of people and being exposed to a greater
variety of ideas and life-styles, Ted began to outgrow his wife. He found it difficult to discuss his
feelings with her or to describe the new goals that
were beginning to take shape in his mind. He
wanted to go back to school so that he could special-
ize in the area of work that he most enjoyed. He also
thought he would like to live abroad for a few years
so that he could learn more about the import-
export end of his business. When he suggested that
they find an apartment of their own and perhaps try
to associate with more friends their own age,
Sharon refused. She was exactly where she wanted
to be: in the bosom of her family. The thought of
moving out into the world—which was so appealing
to Ted—frightened her.

Ted finally had to accept the fact that his wife was
unable to take on the risks of expanding their life.
If he remained with her, it would mean sacrificing
his emerging desires to grow as a person. He would
have to play the child so that his wife could continue
being a child. His answer, ultimately, was No, and
he left both the wife and the family he had outgrown.

When one partner cannot grow, change in the other
partner disrupts the relationship. The static person feels
threatened; because his or her unconscious needs are no
longer being fulfilled by the mate, they may come to the

surface and be exposed—and this is what he wants to avoid. Consequently he fights change or growth in the mate and more or less hands down the ultimatum, "Change *back*—or else!" If this mate could also grow, perhaps the marriage could be saved, but unfortunately this rarely happens. If the more mature partner wants to hold onto his or her chance to develop, he or she usually has to get out of the restrictive marriage.

When one partner is so emotionally disturbed that he or she is unwilling to get help even when that disturbance is pointed out to him or her

People who cannot face their inner needs may deteriorate with time. As the pressures of daily life increase, as these inner needs are more frequently in danger of exposure because of changing life situations, these people may lose their ability to interact with their spouses.

For instance:

ALICE AND BILL

For several years, Alice and Bill had a mother-child relationship. On the surface of their marriage Alice was the long-suffering wife who endured and forgave Bill his outbursts, his extravagance, and his drinking. On the unconscious level of their relationship, however, Bill was the frightened little boy who could always run home to his comforting, mothering wife.

But the drinking got worse over the years because neither Alice nor anyone else could ease Bill's fears that he was not really a man. He sought escape in the bottle. He lost job after job until finally he was unemployable. His children, disgusted and alienated, left home at an early age and refused to see their father.

In seeking help for her husband, Alice began to look at her own relationship with him. She realized that she had played a mothering role in order to avoid the responsibilities of being a wife. While she did everything she could to convince her husband that he needed help with his drinking problem, she had to face the fact that he was unable, or unwilling, to admit that he had a problem. In an effort to salvage what she could of herself and her children, Alice decided to get a divorce.

Why wait?

While it may be hard for a husband or a wife to accept the fact that their marriage is a failure, prolonging the relationship can do a lot of damage, not only to the one who wants out, but also to the one who wants to hold on. When divorce is a need, refusal to acknowledge it only creates or widens the gap between the conscious and unconscious needs of the individual partners. The partner who is growing will be met by resistance each step of the way and eventually his or her self-confidence will break down under constant attack. The partner who resists change will become so deeply entrenched in defense of the role he or she is playing that communication may become impossible. Gradually the relationship becomes a battleground where skirmishes flare over the slightest word, and the only relief is withdrawal from reality.

Even marriage counselors, who traditionally have approached husband-and-wife problems with the determination to save the marriage at all costs, are now finding it more important to save the person. As Dr. Paul Vahanian, psychologist and marriage counselor, put it: "Our job is to help people understand how they are interacting in a relationship. What they choose to do with that understanding is *their* business. They may decide that they simply cannot fulfill each other's needs, and that they should get a divorce. O.K. We are certainly not in the business of gluing them together. A success is when we can facilitate the individuals' learning whatever they need to learn to lead a better life. A failure is when two people go back to the same old life and the same old defenses, and all the pain gets somatized or pushed elsewhere. The marriage may go on . . . but that is a failure."

But what about the children?

Children cannot help being affected by the separation and divorce of their parents. Whether or not they will be emotionally handicapped, however, will depend upon how well or how badly their parents face their own problems.

Being brought up in a one-parent home presents a child with an identity problem, particularly if the parent who leaves is the one with whom the child identified most closely. Then, too, the child feels rejected and abandoned by the absent parent, no matter how frequently they may visit with each other. The child also senses any guilt feelings in this parent and may be confused by them. Stepparents may not be immediately accepted.

In spite of these difficulties, a child of divorced parents does not suffer the emotional agonies of a child in a home that should be broken, but isn't. Parents who stay together "for the sake of the children" are doing them a great disservice and in some cases causing real emotional damage. Because children are extremely sensitive, they know when things aren't going right in the home. They sense hostilities between the parents even when they aren't verbalized. Parents who cannot communicate with each other at all may even use the children to express their pent-up anger for them.

By far the most serious damage these children experience is that they begin to mistrust their own feelings. Sensing that the parents aren't getting along, they may ask what the trouble is—only to be told that there *is* no trouble. Like parents who agree "never to argue in front of the children," these parents are conditioning their children to ignore what they feel because it seems to be wrong, false, or misleading. This, then, is the beginning of a problem that will distort the child's future life as he grows into an adult who has lost touch with himself. Here is where the gap within the self begins.

The best thing parents can do for their children is to level with them and tell them when they are having trouble getting along. By accepting the responsibility for their problems, parents can avoid guilt feelings on the part of the child who thinks he may be the cause of their unhappiness. By acknowledging that their marriage is in trouble, the parents are also enabling the child to rely on what he senses. This may even help the parents to make the decision to separate, if that is what the marriage needs, and it will certainly help the child to live with that decision once it is made.

The disruption of a family is a sad, painful undoing of

many bonds, some of which must be wrenched loose. But the important thing that should be remembered is to *save the person*—whether it be husband, wife, or child. This is the inner need that must be faced.

Uncomplicating the uncoupling

Historically our legal system has been slow to reflect change in human need and social attitudes, and this is particularly true of our divorce laws. Not only are they a maze of whim, prejudice, and misinformation, varying greatly from state to state, but they are based on the outmoded conviction that divorce is a shame and that one of the partners must pay for making it happen. The real reasons for ending the marriage are rarely considered, simply because they do not fit in with the "grounds" for divorce in most states. Therefore, in order to end a marriage, one or both partners often must exaggerate or even lie about details that may have had little to do with the breakup. As one young wife put it, "I wish my husband would hit me in front of a reliable witness, or run around with other women right down the middle of Main Street during lunch hour—just so I could have an easier time getting a divorce."

Hopefully, more states will follow the example of the few that have adopted new divorce laws in which neither partner is blamed for the failure of the marriage. Through these "no-fault" laws, couples can file for a divorce when they no longer can get along together, provided they observe a period of separation. There is no blame, no vilification of one partner through the dishonesty of the other. The marriage is over, and the law, as well as the partners, accepts it.

Beyond making divorce laws more realistic, there should be an updating of the traditions regulating alimony payments and visitation of children. Women have come a long way since the days when they were totally dependent upon their husbands for their support and well-being. Today, if a woman is trained and able to make a living for herself, there is no reason why she should be able to bleed her former husband for alimony, regardless of how much money he may have. This doesn't mean, however, that a man should be able to deprive his children of a decent way of life simply because he no longer lives with their mother.

One of the worst abuses coming out of divorce cases is the ability of a woman to "blackmail" a former husband into paying her more and more money if he wants to see his children. Little is mentioned of this practice when it comes to debates about divorce reform, but the practice is widespread and vicious. Everyone is hurt, but the worst suffering is borne by the children of these broken marriages, who are often told that the reason the absent parent doesn't come to see them is that he doesn't love them anymore.

Facing the truth

Ending a marriage means that one or both partners must face what they have been avoiding—and perhaps why they married in the first place: their real inner needs. Carrying this a step further, it is also what our lawmakers should consider if our divorce laws are to be based upon fairness to both partners in a very unhappy situation. Spouses who blame each other, or their children, or the situations that influence their lives, only perpetuate the gap between their unconscious and conscious desires. In a sense, our irrational divorce laws are a reflection of this inability to face reality. A failure to accept one's self and the real reasons why a marriage has ended may mean that the same failure will be repeated in another marriage or in any intimate relationship. If, however, going through the divorce means that one or both partners can begin to gain some insight into himself or herself, and that they can grow closer to their inner feelings, the experience, while painful, may lead them to a more worthwhile life.

14

Are You Ready for Divorce?—
Ten Questions to Ask Yourself

A young woman who had been through two divorces was planning to marry for the third time. She was optimistic about her chances for success because, as she said, "Everything's different this time." A friend of the family, who had known the young woman for several years, had a different opinion. "Sure—everything's different—except Barbara. She's still looking for a guy who can measure up to Big Daddy." Even though the young woman had married different types of men, she was bringing the same irrational need to each marriage. And she was completely unaware of it.

While divorce may be the most sensible solution to some marriage problems, it's important for the person seeking it to be ready for it. Here again we run into the question of self-understanding: Is the person aware of his or her motives? Or is an unconscious, unrecognized desire calling the shots? If the partner who wants out of a marriage isn't aware of why the marriage went wrong, the same kind of failure can happen again, and again, and again. In this sense, divorce accomplishes nothing. It becomes a game of musical chairs, typified by the actress who, after being married and divorced four times, was asked why she went through the bother of a wedding ceremony. She answered, "I guess I just like things nice and legal."

If your marriage is falling apart, if you no longer want to live with your partner, you owe it to yourself to find out why. Divorce is painful, but it can give you a chance to make a better life for yourself if you're able to learn from your mistakes. Before you can do that, of course, you have to know what those mistakes were.

If you weren't in touch with your feelings when you got married, if you ignored your deeper needs and tried to live up to a conscious image that didn't really express what you wanted out of life—and if your partner did the same thing—you got caught in the marriage gap. One of you changed, or possibly both of you did, and you couldn't satisfy each other any longer. That much you know. That much is evident. But are you aware of what you originally wanted out of marriage? And of how your needs—or your partner's—have changed? And of why those needs can't be fulfilled by either one of you now?

Before you get a divorce, it might be a good idea for you to ask yourself these questions:

1. *What is my part in the problem?*

There is a tendency in a person seeking a divorce to blame the partner for the failure of the marriage. While it often happens that one partner may be less mature, less responsible, more dependent, and less able to accept reality than the other, it still takes two people to break a marriage. For instance, if you're the one who has outgrown your mate, and if your mate lacks the capacity for growth, you still have to face the fact that your development contributed to the marriage breakup. This is not a matter of heaping blame. It's the difference between blaming your mate for not fulfilling your needs and acknowledging that your changing needs, and your partner's unchanging ones, made it impossible for the two of you to interact with each other according to the original terms of your marriage contract.

2. *Have I been using my partner as a parent-figure upon whom I could vent my hostility?*

In some marriages there often is a parent-child or even a brother-sister relationship between the husband and wife. Is this true of your marriage? Have you been playing the parent to a childlike spouse? And do you now need an equal partner? Or have you been the child trying to win from your mate the love and approval you never got from your parents? And are you unhappy with your spouse now because he or she is unable or unwilling to continue playing house with you? Is your partner maturing, and are you unable to grow along with your partner into a more adult husband-and-wife relationship? If this is so, you need to gain more insight into your own needs. Otherwise a divorce will only give you an opportunity to seek the same kind of relationship with someone else and you'll be running the same risk that it will also disappoint you.

3. *Am I blaming my partner for the things that I hate in myself?*

Husbands and wives often blame each other for the inadequacies they can't face in themselves. Do you, for instance, feel that your mate is a passive, unambitious, ineffective, dependent mouse? And is he or she really that kind of person? Or are *you* the one who unconsciously feels inadequate? Perhaps you deliberately chose a passive mate so that you could have an outlet for your own self-hatred. If this is so, and you can't face your own shortcomings, another marriage relationship will probably turn out the same way.

4. *Would things really be different with another partner?*

If your marriage is in trouble because you aren't aware of your unconscious needs, chances are you'll run into the same difficulties with another partner. Unconsciously you may want people to walk all over you. Unconsciously you may resent men because your father was a tyrant, or you may have contempt for women because your mother was a pushover. Maybe you're defensive because your brothers and sisters picked on you. As long as these or other feelings aren't faced squarely and brought to the surface where they can be worked out or expressed as part of the real you, they'll seek gratification in subtle, confusing ways.

Are you having the same kind of problems getting along with your boss or your friends that you have with your mate? If so, changing marriage partners probably won't improve your chances for happiness. You need to look more deeply into yourself and try to understand who you really are and what you want from life.

5. *Am I looking for a way out to justify my extramarital affair?*

Do you feel guilty because you're having an affair? And can you face your guilt? Is the person with whom you're having the affair someone who can fulfill your real needs? Can you fulfill his or hers? Were you driven into the affair by frustration in your marriage rather than by a feeling of satisfaction from the other person? Or possibly to prove to yourself that you're a desirable person? Are you willing to explore your reasons for seeking satisfaction from someone other than your mate? Do you want to know what's wrong with your marriage? Or are you pressing for a divorce so that you won't have to deal with these problems? In other words, are you having the affair to satisfy your unfulfilled needs—or to avoid facing them?

6. *Am I trying to justify the narcissistic demands I make on my partner?*

Do you feel that your mate and children "deprived" you of the better things in life? Do you ever tell your wife and children (of course, you always say you're kidding) that you'd be a rich man if you didn't have to support them? Or do you tell your husband and children how much fun you could have if they didn't tie you down? Well, maybe you're not kidding. Unconsciously you may really mean it. And now perhaps you think you can escape to that Never-Never Land where everything is yours alone.

But before you leave, think about this: Nobody forced you to get married. Nobody said you *had* to have a family. In spite of all your protests, you made those decisions on your own. Your family is stuck with you just as much as you're stuck with them. Perhaps you had better ask yourself whether you can have a relationship with anyone without giving something of yourself to it.

7. *Am I running away from responsibility?*

Do you find yourself reminiscing about your school days? Do you wish you could turn the clock back to a time when you didn't have a worry in the world? Would you like to join the Pepsi Generation and hang loose? Join a commune? Go to a pot party? In fact, is that the kind of life you're trying to live?

Are the demands of marriage and parenthood more than you can handle? Are you—perhaps unconsciously—afraid that you're more a child than an adult? Are your mate and children asking too much of you? And do you really think you'll have fewer responsibilities if you're on your own?

If you haven't developed the capacity to handle adult responsibilities, you may be trying to run away from yourself instead of your partner.

8. *Am I trying to avoid the fact that I'm getting older?*

A husband and wife who have been married several years confront each other daily with the reminder that they're not as young as they used to be. If one of them can't accept this reality, if one of them sees himself or herself as a child and wants to remain that way, he or she may try to preserve that image by seeking a new and younger mate.

If you and your partner have been married a long time and you suddenly find that your relationship is empty, there may be reasons other than age. Perhaps you were too wrapped up in your children to notice that your needs weren't being fulfilled by your mate. Or you may expect your mate to fill the void left by children who have grown up. Or it may have taken you this long to outgrow your partner. But you *may* just be afraid of getting older. If you are, changing your partner won't change your age.

9. *Is there real evidence that I am more mature and more stable than my partner? Am I sure my partner is unwilling or unable to change?*

It's unreasonable to expect young couples to be fully developed when they marry. They should, however, have a pretty good idea of what they want from life and especially from a husband or a wife. What really counts in a young marriage is the partners' growth potential. Can each of them develop? Is each one flexible enough to accept and adapt to growth changes in the other? These are the questions to ask yourself now if it seems that one of you may be outgrowing the other.

For instance, if you're the one who feels more responsible and independent, and if you get stuck making all the decisions, you ought to consider whether this is a temporary readjustment or the permanent direction your marriage is taking. Is your mate the kind of person who can grow? Or is he or she trying to stop you from growing because it means you won't continue to satisfy some of his or her needs? Have you talked about your feelings with your partner? Is he or she considerate of your changing needs and does he or she make an effort to satisfy them? Or does your mate complain that you're not the same person he or she married? Does your mate want you to "change back"? Can your mate bring his or her feelings into the open and tell you how he or she reacts to your new needs? Can he or she admit to fears and apprehensions? Is your mate aware that some of these fears may be childish? Can he or she laugh at some of them once they become known?

Can *you* be open and honest with your partner? Can *you* bring your feelings to the surface and express them without fear of disapproval or rejection? When you realize that some of your attitudes are immature or irrational, can you explore yourself a bit further to find the reasons for them?

If either of you has a serious emotional problem that you can't resolve on your own, are you willing to seek help for it? This is very important because it indicates whether you and your partner really want to grow and develop or simply *say* that you do.

If you are impatient because you expect your partner to grow and change at the same pace and in precisely the same ways that you are changing, then *you* may be the one who is inflexible and unable to adapt to the needs of another person. But if your partner is not in touch with his or her own needs, then your partner certainly won't be in touch with yours. You're better off realizing this right now.

10. *Would I grow on my own?*

How do you feel about being on your own? Does it scare you? Do you think you can make it? Do you keep throwing obstacles in your own way?

If you're afraid of being on your own, if you'd rather endure the frustrations of an unsatisfying marriage than take your chances on making a better life for yourself, then you haven't really grown up. You're also making unfair and unrealistic demands upon your partner, and this may be why your marriage is coming apart.

Actually, each and every one of us is alone, in a sense. Each of us should be able to stand on his or her own two feet. In a marriage, a man and a woman cooperate. They share and combine their abilities to make a life for themselves. But each *should* be able to function well as an individual whenever that is necessary. In other words, you have to be able to function well on your own before you can function well as a married person.

Divorce is neither good nor bad in itself. It is advisable or inadvisable, depending upon the circumstances of the marriage and the readiness of the person who wants out of the marriage. The point to be made is: If you didn't marry with your eyes wide open, be sure that you know what you're doing—and *why*—when you get a divorce.

PART

V

NARROWING THE MARRIAGE GAP

15

Other Forms of Intimacy

A young man whose marriage was breaking up told his lawyer that he realized at the time of his wedding that he wasn't ready for marriage. "I wasn't especially wild about the girl I was marrying, either. But I was attracted to her —physically, I guess you could say—and I was tired of being alone. What else can a guy do?"

Many young men and women have done the same thing. Urged into marriage by loneliness, sexual desire, or an eagerness to be independent of parents, and without any clear understanding of what they want from a partner, they are more likely to settle for a mate who appeals only to their infantile needs. And as the young man said, "What else can a guy do?" Or a girl, for that matter?

Suggesting that young people wait until they know themselves better before they marry may be sound advice, but it's hard to follow. What do people do for intimacy while they are developing?

The answer depends upon the person and whether or

not he is aware of his inner needs. In Chapter 4, we discussed a young couple who chose to live together so that they could enjoy a form of intimacy that was less demanding than marriage. They weren't able to assume a greater responsibility and they knew it, but they didn't fool themselves into believing that living together was a substitute for a more committed relationship. It was simply the one that suited their mutual needs at the time.

Another couple we discussed were living together without any awareness of their inner feelings. To them their arrangement was a substitute for marriage, which they considered an obsolete relationship. Actually they were ready neither for marriage nor for the relationship they attempted to form. The conflict between their conscious and unconscious needs, which they were unable to face, was destroying their union as surely as it has destroyed many marriages.

Marriage has never been the *only* form of intimate relationship. There have always been alternatives, but only now are they becoming socially acceptable. The man and woman who live together today are not ostracized. If they choose, they can have children and live as a family without fear of social reprisals from those who disapprove of their way of life. Groups of men and women, most of them young, are openly experimenting with communal life. In other words, the world is hanging loose as far as human intimacy is concerned.

In whichever ways men and women relate, however, they will be seeking to satisfy their basic desires through each other. Whether they live together without commitment or with it, as a couple or as members of a communal family, or perhaps as a single person, they will be asking the same things of each other. Their needs will draw them together, and their frustrations will drive them apart.

Why get married at all?

Some men and women never marry, nor do they live with a partner. They remain single and unattached all their lives. Quite often they are very close to their parents, but even after the parents die, there is no change in the solitary life of the children.

Many single people say that they'd like to be married, but that the "right one" never came along. Some say that the one person they loved turned them down and they don't want to get hurt again. Some are aggressively independent, insisting that they don't need anyone but themselves. They also don't admire what they see in the marriages of their friends.

The concern about overpopulation and the availability of birth control devices are also causing some men and women to question the need for a partner in their lives. They feel they can satisfy their needs better than anyone else can, and they point to the high divorce rate as a poor argument in favor of sharing.

Years ago "spinster" and "bachelor" were uncomfortable labels. No one knew what to do with these people who seemed to lack a desire for a home and family of their own. To avoid being considered "odd," many young men and women rushed into unhappy marriages.

Now the situation has changed. Very often the unattached, freewheeling, on-the-go man or woman is envied, especially by those who have had frustrating experiences in marriage. With a good job, the chance to travel and do as you please, an apartment of one's own and enough money to buy what you want, who needs anyone else?

While the single life may have its appeal, there's a lot more to it than a determination to be independent and individual or to avoid the discomfort of unrequited love. Quite possibly the perennial bachelor or career girl can't exchange vows with a mate because their vows have already been exchanged with their parents. In many families the child makes an unconscious agreement never to leave the parents. They satisfy one another's inner needs, the child's to remain dependent and the parents' to baby the child. There is no provision for another partner.

In spite of their insistence that marriage is stifling and that an affair isn't much better, many single people don't marry because they're afraid to get close to someone. They are unable to meet another person on a deep emotional level because their own emotions have never developed beyond those of the child. They hold onto their parents because unconsciously they feel no one else can love them, and they doubt their own capacity to love. Being fearful of involvement, they try to defend themselves against it by damning it.

Let's all live together

One of the most interesting experiments in intimacy is the commune. Actually a commune can be many things, depending upon the needs of the members. Usually it is a group of men and women who live as a family. In some communes the men and women do not pair off in couples. In others, they are a family of couples, married or unmarried, who share a home, a way of life, and their economic resources. Their children may be brought up as children of the whole group rather than as offspring of the individual couples. There may be an attempt to structure the group along traditional family lines, with one member acting as a father to the others, or they all may live as brothers and sisters, children in the family of mankind. In some communes no sexual relationships are permitted, in some the couples practice sexual fidelity, and in some the sexual relationships are shared openly.

Communal living, according to its members, is an attempt to get away from the pressures of a technological society, from its meaningless jobs, its overpopulated areas, and its alienated individuals. Most commune members say that they are trying to return to the essentials of human life. In their eyes they are exchanging a slick, materialistic existence for a way of life that offers them close contact with people who care about them. The badge of their contempt for the rat race is their simple, frugal, often impoverished level of life. They give their time to the "family," working outside it only when they have to and at whatever jobs are available to them.

At first, communes were considered a joke. In their efforts to reduce their material needs, the families wore clothing and ate foods that seemed bizarre. In reality their clothes were hand-me-downs and their food was cheap and in many instances nourishing. They let their hair grow to avoid the expense of barbers. The charge that all of them were filthy was exaggerated. The filthy ones simply stood out.

Now that their existence has become more acceptable to many people, communes are becoming more interesting as experiments in human relationships. With the breakdown of many marriages and the fragmentation of so many homes more people are fearful that the family will become extinct. The commune's aim is to revive it.

Some observers of these families feel that they are the wave of the future. This, they say, is the younger generation's successful flight from the grip of a dehumanized society. Here, they say, is where a man and a woman are free to touch each other, to lean upon each other, to count on the support of each other—and because they want to, not because they must. Here, they also say, is where the individual can live in close relationship to more than *one* other individual. Here is where he can experience the family relationships that modern living stifles. Marriage, to commune members and their advocates, has become a cell in which two people are cut off from the warmth of contact with other human beings.

To the young, communes offer more than an escape from the Establishment. They offer a version of family life, something many young people have never experienced. A great many of them have seen their parents separate and perhaps take new partners. They have known their fathers only between business trips. They have seen their mothers become lonely, frustrated women, uncertain of their function in life and resentful of the children they have had to bring up with little help from their husbands.

In spite of the claims that the commune is the life-style of the future, it can also be interpreted as regressive. As participants in a group, commune members are more childlike and more dependent; they bend more to the pressures to conform rather than developing the distinctive features of the individual.

If anything, communes are symptoms of family breakdowns, not solutions to them. The young people who gather to live together, hoping to find the parental support they missed as children, cannot possibly know what a real family is. Not having had one, their expectations are extravagant, idealistic, and immature. At the same time they are resentful of authority, especially if it is imperfect. As the group takes shape, as some members emerge as parental figures and some as children, hostilities flare. There are sexual jealousies and arguments over child-rearing. When a lot of people live together, they get on each other's nerves. This is one of the reasons why we grow away from our families as we develop. The development of a new family unit is the natural thrust of maturity. Seeking to become part of an artificially structured family is an attempt to escape from adult life and reenter the womb. It can't be done.

In practice, communes haven't been successful. Most of them disband within a short time, and within those that survive for a longer period of time, the turnover is rapid. Most of the people who join communes can't take that kind of life very long. As much as they want to seek peace, love, brotherhood, and unselfish sharing of all they have, they are still human beings who want to go their own way and have their own things. They are not free to be themselves since they must now conform to the structure of the communal group rather than to a particular level of the Establishment. In this sense, they are not dropping any façade by fleeing the pressures of society; they are only exchanging one façade for another. The only way these men and women can ever become free is to rebuild the lines of communication between their feelings and their behavior. They are as far from doing that in a commune as they were back in the rat race.

Let's try it out

Some couples are living together without marrying because, as a popular singer recently put it, "They don't want to get stuck with a lemon for life." Reluctant to depend solely on their emotions in choosing a mate, these couples want to try each other out in a more practical manner and discover how they react to each other on a day-to-day basis. Better contraceptives now make it possible for men and women to do this without taking on the responsibility, or the risk, of having children.

Living together is as close as a couple can come to marriage without making a legal commitment. But that commitment is an important omission. For instance, the man and woman who live together in free union aren't bound to stand by each other in sickness and in health, for richer or poorer. They are free to leave at any time and without any obligation to each other. They also take on no responsibility for each other. For some men and women this is an element of insecurity.

Living together does give a couple a chance to react to each other's needs, and very often they discover certain desires in themselves that emerge only within the intimacy of close association. It also gives them a chance to recover from the initial impact of sexual attraction and fulfillment so that their erotic needs will not obscure their other desires in life.

Free unions rarely are permanent living arrangements. They may be, if one or both partners is legally bound to another partner who won't consent to a divorce. Otherwise, they usually are preliminary relationships. If the partners find that their needs and desires intermesh, they will usually want to make their relationship legal and binding after a while.

Today, however, free union is incorrectly used to describe repetitive relationships that don't necessarily last long. Some men and women live with one partner after another, for a few weeks or months at a time. They may begin a relationship vowing that they will never become serious about each other. Their plan is to live together but to lead separate lives as well, with no obligation to either partner. They will enjoy but not feel, and as long as they stay that way, the arrangement works. Sooner or later, however, one partner may begin to feel more deeply in need of the other, and that is when the relationship may end. Playing in the house is fun, but living in it is threatening.

It is obvious that couples who prefer these short-term arrangements to marriage, or even to a more lasting free union, want to avoid making commitments to each other. While they claim to value their independence and individuality, they may actually be motivated by the fear that they are not lovable. If a person is convinced that no one wants him, he will try to protect himself from rejection by not getting deeply involved with someone. Intimacy becomes something to be avoided, and ironically the expression of love from a partner is seen as an approaching put-down. The threatened partner is saying, "I know you only want to get close to me so that you can reject me. I can't stand that, it hurts too much. I'm getting out of here!" But because the partner is a human being, and because all human beings need closeness with other human beings, he or she will continue to seek it in other relationships. Of necessity, these people will choose partners who are also afraid of rejection so that they can make the same vows to keep their emotional distance from each other.

The sad part of it is that the rejection will come only if either partner reaches for the other out of love.

Options within a marriage

Not all unhappy couples get divorced. Some are convinced that it wouldn't do them any good and wouldn't be worth the expense. Because they may doubt their ability to satisfy their needs through another person, they agree to maintain the marriage and ignore it at the same time. Husband and wife go their separate ways, socially, financially, and often sexually.

There are couples who say that this is the only way to live because it allows them to remain independent and at the same time satisfies their need for companionship. In their eyes, the more traditional forms of marriage demand that one partner, usually the woman, give up a lot of herself to meet the demands of the other, usually the man. They insist they they would suffocate in such a relationship, and if they cannot do as they please with their partner, they choose to do it alone. Marriage, for these couples, is a nonbinding, uncommitted form of friendship.

Sex on the side

While infidelity is not always a feature of the "go-it-alone" marriage, it frequently becomes unavoidable. When married men or women consistently show up alone at parties and other social events, they don't exactly hide in a corner. Even if they aren't trying to attract another woman or man, it's likely to happen. One of the reasons is that husbands and wives who live separate lives usually have unsatisfied needs, and sex is one of them. While both partners in these marriages may consciously intend merely to spend a companionable few hours with someone of the opposite sex, these platonic relationships are often disrupted by their unconscious needs. If, unconsciously, the wife and husband have unfed sexual longings, no amount of rules laid down with a new acquaintance is going to keep those longings from being fed once food is in sight.

Infidelity is sometimes sought after and becomes an accepted part of an unhappy marriage. As we mentioned in Chapter 4, an important ritual in this kind of infidelity is the rehashing of it, in minute detail, between the husband and wife.

In some groups of married couples, husband-and-wife-swapping has become institutionalized. Group sex, in which everyone does it with everyone else's mate, and all at the same time, is claimed by some to be a great revitalizer for a sagging marriage. Its practitioners say that the sexual variety and openness improve the sex life of a husband and wife. Here, again, the partners describe their sexual experiences to each other, comparing techniques and degrees of erotic excitation of the lovers and the mates.

Room to grow?

Intimacy on a meaningful level doesn't stifle the individuality of either spouse; in fact, a marriage should make it possible for each partner to grow and reach his and her greatest potential. There is nothing more stimulating or fulfilling to the human personality than an environment of love and acceptance, respect, support, communication of needs, and the satisfaction of those needs on both the conscious and unconscious levels.

Giving and taking, sharing and being shared with, pleasing and being pleased—these are fundamental characteristics of intimate relationships. If one partner in a marriage is doing the giving while the other is taking it all, or if one partner must shine at the expense of the other, then we're not talking about a good marriage. Neither can we judge all other marriages on this basis. The open-marriage arrangement prescribes a form of behavior without acknowledging the gut human needs and ignores the most basic desires and motivations. It enables a husband and wife to live together like two roommates who don't know each other very well. While the advocates of open marriage stress the advantages of individuality, in actual practice, the stress is upon superficiality in the relationship.

The wife who constantly goes alone to concerts because her husband doesn't like classical music, the husband who always goes off with the boys on fishing trips because his wife can't stand the sight of worms, are not "making their marriage work." They are prolonging its demise, perhaps because they may feel they wouldn't do any better with another partner. They are ignoring their unmet inner needs, not feeding them, and eventually these appetites will make themselves known in uncomfortable ways. The husband or wife who won't share at least some of the other's interests has a problem. Perhaps he or she is unable to get close to another person, or can't give something of himself or herself.

Couples who practice infidelity as part of married life

are usually expressing their inability to find satisfaction (more often emotional than sexual) with their mate. Sexual promiscuity in these marriages is also often a coverup for repressed and misunderstood homosexual longings such as those that were described in Chapter 8. The same may be true for group sex.

In a dynamic marriage the sexual satisfaction of both partners expands and deepens. As they explore each other's erotic needs, and as they find themselves able to please each other to a greater and greater degree, both their desires and their satisfactions will increase. Here, too, there is no wide gap between what these partners are and what they think they ought to be. They act out their feelings of love and erotic stimulation, unafraid to give themselves to the partner, grateful for the pleasure they are receiving, strengthened rather than shattered by their intimacy and commitment.

If two people are fulfilling each other sexually, there isn't room for a third party. But if they aren't getting what they want, infidelity won't supply it either. We can't ignore the fact that human emotions run very deep. A man and a woman can't sleep with other partners and expect their marriage to go on as if nothing had happened. If it does, then the infidelity itself may be feeding some of the couple's repressed desires, perhaps even the desire to be betrayed and humiliated.

Attempting to make infidelity a part of marriage is institutionalizing the partners' inability to feel. It's as if they were saying, "This marriage is already dead, so let's do the things that ordinarily would have killed it." Rather than reviving a marriage, it dances on its grave.

The great escape

Any one of these other forms of intimacy can be a satisfactory temporary living arrangement for the person who is not ready for marriage *and knows it.* They may, in fact, provide some of the human experiences through which we become aware of our needs. But if they are viewed as a substitute for marriage, and if couples enter into them with the same lack of self-understanding they bring to so many marriages, the results will be painfully disappointing. Nor will there be much of a chance for growth during the relationship because the couple will be rigidly locked into the same positions they would have taken in premature marriages. Only the legal entanglements are avoided.

Throwing marriage out and trying something else in its place is putting the emphasis on the wrong part of the problem. Men and women *are* having greater difficulty in their attempted relationships; they *are* finding it harder and harder to give each other the deep comfort and security that comes from fulfilled desires. But the trouble originates from inside themselves, not from outside. Our society and its accelerating pace aggravates our interpersonal frustrations, but doesn't create them. Changing our environment may ease the stress, but it won't remove the problems. On the other hand, if more men and women were able to work out their inner conflicts, if they were able to behave in a manner based upon trust in their feelings, they would no doubt be able to reduce the social pressures to a level they could tolerate. People who know who they are and what they want are able to live the way they want. Technology becomes their tool, not their master.

Today men and women are telling each other to "do

their thing," but do they mean it? In order to do their thing, they have to feel it first. It's the same with their relationships. Human beings can't get close to each other until they drop the façade that hides what they are. Men and women have to *be* their thing before they can do it. Marriage, or any other form of intimacy, will work only when they become themselves.

16

Closing the Gap Within the Self

If growth and self-awareness are the keys to a happy marriage, how, then, can these be achieved? How can men and women get more in touch with their inner needs so that they can express them openly and get what they really want out of life? The answer, of course, will depend upon the person, his age, his circumstances, and his potential for growth.

It's easy to tell an eighteen-year-old to wait until he's mature enough to marry. A thirty-year-old is another matter. The younger the person is, the easier it is for him to change old patterns of behavior as new needs are realized. An older person has had more years to reinforce the façade behind which he hides from his unconscious feelings. He defends himself much more vigorously against change, and the recognition of his needs is therefore a longer, slower, more uncomfortable process. Nevertheless, it can be done—and has been, by many men and women.

It's also easier for a single person to work toward change. A husband or wife, faced with the possibility that one partner's growth may disrupt or destroy a marriage, has a hard choice to make. But the development of either partner may be their only chance for a happy, productive life, and they would be wise to take advantage of it. Many husbands and wives have.

How does a person grow?

Life is the soil in which a person develops. As we go through the experiences of living—acting and reacting to situations and to other persons and being influenced by them—we change. As we perceive how people respond to us, to the things we do and say and feel; as we examine the consequences of our actions, our choices and our decisions, we become aware of who we are.

Of course, this is not true of everyone. For some people the word *experience* might be defined as "gaining practice in making the same old mistakes again and again." Instead of examining their behavior to find out how they may have helped to create the situations that repeatedly bring them rejection, failure, humiliation, disappointment and pain, they keep trying to justify their status quo. For these people some form of therapy might be needed to help them look into themselves.

But for the person who has the ability to look at himself objectively, growth is a matter of time and self-awareness. This person evaluates the way he behaves and the way others react to him. If he finds himself acting in a way that repeatedly frustrates him, he looks into his motivations. Once he learns what his inner needs are, he brings them into his conscious mind by expressing them through his actions. Gradually, as he becomes more familiar with himself, he ceases to behave in ways that conflict with his inner emotions, and his sense of frustration leaves him.

What the maturing person doesn't learn for himself he learns through others. An older brother or a sister, a parent, a friend, a teacher, or a clergyman—someone with understanding—may be able to point out when a person is doing something childish. And instead of defending himself against this criticism, such a person holds it up to himself to see whether it might provide him with a clue to his real identity. If he *is* behaving childishly, he wants to know why and he wants to change.

A person can learn a lot from his mistakes, especially if he's willing to admit them. He may not like the way he behaves in a particular situation or toward a particular person, and if he explores the emotions that prompted his actions, he may find that they were irrational. By being aware of them he may be able to change.

We also learn about ourselves through some of the painful events in life. A disappointing love affair, the death of a loved one, a bad marriage, or a divorce may bring some of our inner feelings to the surface, and if a person is willing to explore them he can get closer to his basic needs. The same is true of other significant events, such as the birth of a child. Even social forces, such as the women's movement or a major political trend may cause us to sense emotions we didn't know we had. The person who can evaluate these feelings in himself can grow.

Pay attention to your fantasies

Has a thought ever raced through your mind so quickly that it disappears almost before you're aware of it? What do you do about it? Do you catch it and hold onto it, or do you say, "Oh, well, it's probably not important," and let it go? Most people let these thoughts go, and they really shouldn't, because they are extremely important. They may hold the keys to the door between a person's conscious and unconscious needs.

What do you do about your daydreams? And your fantasies? Do you explore them? Or do you push them out of your mind because you're embarrassed or frightened by them? They are valuable guides to your inner feelings and you shouldn't dismiss them—or, worse yet, repress them.

It is through these fleeting thoughts and wishes and fantasies that our unconscious needs are communicated, and the person who wants to get acquainted with himself or herself should pay close attention to them.

What do they mean?

Fantasies, daydreams, and fleeting thoughts aren't always what they seem to be, so don't go by first impressions. It may take some insight to understand what they are communicating.

For example:

WAYNE

For a long time Wayne had been daydreaming about his high school days, and it bothered him. What did it mean? Was he afraid of getting old? Did he want to leave his wife and children? These possibilities alarmed him so much that he tried to keep nostalgic thoughts out of his mind.

As his fantasies recurred, Wayne became irritable, especially when he was home with his family. He felt guilty about the possibility that he might not love them, yet he had no real indication that this was true.

If Wayne had continued to censor his fantasies, the pressures arising from his resistance to them might have caused a serious problem in his marriage. He also might have continued to live in conflict with the needs that his fantasies were trying to communicate to him. Instead, Wayne took a long, hard look at his nostalgic daydreams. By thinking about them objectively, he brought them into his conscious mind, where he held them up against the realities of his life. What was it about his high school days that held such an attraction for him now? He didn't really want to be a teen-ager again, and he loved his wife and children very much, so they weren't the cause of his discomfort. But when you're a teen-ager, you don't have a lot of responsibilities, and yes, that was it! Wayne *felt* the answer by paying attention to the emotions his daydreams aroused in him as he thought about them consciously. He realized he was overburdened with financial problems and recently he had been promoted to a job that required a kind of training he lacked. While he couldn't admit his frustrations consciously, his unconscious feelings were signaling their distress through his fantasies, through sudden images of days when he didn't have a worry in the world. Clearly, he wanted to get out from under.

Once Wayne understood how he felt about his life, he was in a position to make some changes in it. He was able to solve his financial problems by reducing his living costs, and he decided to go to school at night to get the training he needed to do his job well.

LOUANN

Quite unexpectedly, Louann began having sexual fantasies about men she hardly knew. She felt guilty about this because she thought it indicated that she wanted to be unfaithful to her husband.

This kind of misinterpretation might have led Louann into an affair, or at least it might have caused some conflict in her marriage. Fortunately, Louann was a woman who could look at herself critically. She knew she loved her husband and that they had a very good sex life. Then she realized that her fantasies came during the times when she was tense. She saw that they were not expressing a desire to be promiscuous or a dissatisfaction with her husband. They were simply signaling her need for sexual relief from some of the stresses of her life. It was this understanding that helped Louann to realize that she and her husband could ease their inner tensions as well as express their passion and love through their sexual relationship.

NOREEN

When Noreen's husband was away for a few days on a business trip, she worried about him constantly. At night she kept imagining him in an accident. In some of her fantasies he was dead. These grim thoughts disturbed her. Did she really want some harm to come to her husband?

Gradually Noreen began to look at her fantasies more closely, paying particular attention to the way she felt when she was daydreaming. She saw, then, that she had no hostility toward her husband. In fact, when she imagined that he was dead she felt like a child crying out, "I wish you'd die!" because she wanted to become independent of an ever-present parent. Noreen did want to be independent. She wanted to do something meaningful in her life, yet she was afraid to go out in the world and test her abilities. To avoid facing her inner fears, in her conscious mind she began to blame her husband for tying her down and depriving her of an opportunity to have a more meaningful life. Her fantasies, however, continued to communicate her unconscious needs to her.

When Noreen was able to face her fears, she realized that she was blaming her husband for her own inadequacies and her fears of responsibility. It was these, rather than her husband, that restricted her, and so she wished them "dead."

Once she could accept how she felt, Noreen could

do something about her life. With her husband's help she worked out a plan to take a part-time job that would give her a chance to take on responsibility slowly, allowing her time to adjust to a more independent way of life.

Becoming acquainted with one's feelings is the first step a person should take toward maturity. Communicating these feelings through one's behavior is the second and crucial step. It takes time, and mistakes will be made. But such a person will be more likely to catch himself in the act when he is repeating an old pattern of behavior that is in conflict with his inner needs. By recalling his needs consciously, he usually can express them in a way that will lead to fulfillment rather than frustration.

Getting in touch with life

Every now and then a man or a woman comes to a therapist to "solve a marriage problem." Of course, it can't be done, because there are no "marriage problems." There are only human problems—the frustrations, unrealistic expectations, and repressed desires that are born of the conflict between a person's conscious and unconscious needs. These a man and a woman bring with them into marriage, and they can be solved only by dealing with the whole person, not just his or her marriage. For marriage cannot be separated from the rest of life, and the way a person approaches his life is the way he'll approach his marriage.

When a person is in touch with himself and can express his genuine needs, other things in his life seem to fall into line. Being tuned in to his own emotions and needs makes him more sensitive to the feelings and needs of others, and he reacts to people on a deeper, more intimate level. Usually he will have a stimulating, productive life and successful relationships; he'll do the kind of work he enjoys and, above all, he'll have a happy, fulfilling marriage. But when a person has inner conflicts that blind him to his basic needs, very little in his life seems to work out well. The frustrations in one area of his life seem to spill over into all the others. Being a guarded person who avoids facing himself, he also meets others on a superficial, meaningless level. He's afraid of intimacy because it may strip him of his defenses.

There are choices in life. As complex as our society has become, as rapidly as we experience change and obsolescence, we can still select from life the things that best suit our individual needs. We can take from the world whatever we need to build our personal environment and reject whatever is useless or alien.

The unaware person has no such choice, because he doesn't know what he wants. Driven by needs he isn't aware of, attempting to cover up emotions he vaguely senses but cannot accept, he is often most miserable when he gets what he thinks he wants—but really doesn't. Unable to create his own environment, he is fragmented and confused by the choices available to him. He would rather squeeze himself into a mold in which he could remain fixed, immobile, for the rest of his life. That, however, is the one choice not open to him.

The right partners

The chances of success in marriage depend upon our ability to narrow the gap between the conscious and unconscious needs of the husband and wife. If the partners are flexible people who can grow, if they can learn about themselves and each other by paying attention to their feelings, and if they can express these feelings so that their needs are clearly communicated to each other, they won't be torn apart by problems arising from within themselves. And they will be much better able to deal with any problems on the outside.

In a world where the integrity of political leaders, heads of state and law enforcement officials is being questioned, where the values of the past generation have been rejected as false, where the familiar may become obsolete overnight, where relationships are quickly formed and just as quickly ended, it is hard for us to trust one another.

We can trust each other only when we know what lies beneath the surface. We have to get close and contact each other's inner feelings. In order to do this, our feelings have to be freely expressed. If they aren't, we can fool ourselves and make mistakes; we find ourselves forced into premature, reckless behavior by the needs we can't express. How much better it is to be free of them, to be able to make a real choice among all the opportunities life offers us. How much better it is to know ourselves so that we can know others, to have nothing to hide or to hide from. What better guide can we have in this world than our feelings? What greater happiness can we have than the fulfillment of the needs that make us what we are?

A good marriage can offer a man and a woman the kind of trusting intimacy they need to sustain them in an uncertain world. It provides them with an environment in which they can be themselves and communicate their deepest desires. Each recognizes and confirms what the other is; each says to the other, "Yes, I can see what you are, and I love you very much *because* you are what you are. I can depend on you to be what you appear to be. I don't have to fear that as I discover more of you, you will disappoint me or betray me. You are genuine."

Index

245

Index